IMMERSION
Bible Studies

JOSHUA
JUDGES
RUTH

Praise for IMMERSION

"IMMERSION BIBLE STUDIES is a godsend for participants who desire sound Bible study yet feel they do not have large amounts of time for study and preparation. IMMERSION is concise. It is brief but covers the material well and leads participants to apply the Bible to life. IMMERSION is a wonderful resource for today's church."

Larry R. Baird, senior pastor of Trinity Grand Island United Methodist Church

"If you're looking for a deeper knowledge and understanding of God's Word, you must dive into IMMERSION BIBLE STUDIES. Whether in a group setting or as an individual, you will experience God and his unconditional love for each of us in a whole new way."

Pete Wilson, founding and senior pastor of Cross Point Church

"This beautiful series helps readers become fluent in the words and thoughts of God, for purposes of illumination, strength building, and developing a closer walk with the One who loves us so."

Laurie Beth Jones, author of *Jesus, CEO* and *The Path*

"The IMMERSION BIBLE STUDIES series is no less than a game changer. It ignites the purpose and power of Scripture by showing us how to do more than just know God or love God; it gives us the tools to love like God as well."

Shane Stanford, author of *You Can't Do Everything . . . So Do Something*

"I highly commend to you IMMERSION BIBLE STUDIES, which tells us what the Bible teaches and how to apply it personally."

John Ed Mathison, author of *Treasures of the Transformed Life*

IMMERSION
Bible Studies

JOSHUA

JUDGES

RUTH

Isabel N. Docampo

Abingdon Press

Nashville

JOSHUA, JUDGES, RUTH
IMMERSION BIBLE STUDIES
by Isabel N. Docampo

Copyright © 2012 by Abingdon Press

Library of Congress Cataloging-in-Publication Data

Docampo, Isabel N., 1955-
  Joshua, Judges, Ruth / Isabel N. Docampo.
    pages cm — (Immersion Bible studies)
  ISBN 978-1-4267-1634-8 (curriculum—printed / text plus-cover : alk. paper) 1. Bible. O.T.
Joshua—Textbooks. 2. Bible. O.T. Judges—Textbooks. 3. Bible. O.T. Ruth—Textbooks. I. Title.
  BS1295.55.D63 2012
  222'.06—dc23

                                                                                    2012018256

Editor: Stan Purdum
Leader Guide Writer: Martha Bettis Gee

12 13 14 15 16 17 18 19 20 21—10 9 8 7 6 5 4 3 2 1

Manufactured in the United States of America

Contents

REVIEW TEAM

Diane Blum
Pastor
East End United Methodist Church
Nashville, Tennessee

Susan Cox
Pastor
McMurry United Methodist Church
Claycomo, Missouri

Margaret Ann Crain
Professor of Christian Education
Garrett-Evangelical Theological Seminary
Evanston, Illinois

Nan Duerling
Curriculum Writer and Editor
Cambridge, Maryland

Paul Escamilla
Pastor and Writer
St. John's United Methodist Church
Austin, Texas

James Hawkins
Pastor and Writer
Smyrna, Delaware

Andrew Johnson
Professor of New Testament
Nazarene Theological Seminary
Kansas City, Missouri

Snehlata Patel
Pastor
Woodrow United Methodist Church
Staten Island, New York

Emerson B. Powery
Professor of New Testament
Messiah College
Grantham, Pennsylvania

Clayton Smith
Pastoral Staff
Church of the Resurrection
Leawood, Kansas

Harold Washington
Professor of Hebrew Bible
Saint Paul School of Theology
Kansas City, Missouri

Carol Wehrheim
Curriculum Writer and Editor
Princeton, New Jersey

Immersion Bible Studies

*A fresh new look at the Bible, from beginning to end,
and what it means in your life.*

Welcome to Immersion!

We've asked some of the leading Bible scholars, teachers, and pastors to help us with a new kind of Bible study. Immersion remains true to Scripture but always asks, "Where are you in your life? What do you struggle with? What makes you rejoice?" Then it helps you read the Scriptures to discover their deep, abiding truths. Immersion is about God and God's Word, and it is also about you—not just your thoughts, but your feelings and your faith.

In each study you will prayerfully read the Scripture and reflect on it. Then you will engage it in three ways:

Claim Your Story
Through stories and questions, think about your life, with its struggles and joys.

Enter the Bible Story
Explore Scripture and consider what God is saying to you.

Live the Story
Reflect on what you have discovered, and put it into practice in your life.

IMMERSION makes use of an exciting new translation of Scripture, the Common English Bible (CEB). The CEB and IMMERSION BIBLE STUDIES will offer adults:

- the emotional expectation to find the love of God
- the rational expectation to find the knowledge of God
- reliable, genuine, and credible power to transform lives
- clarity of language

Whether you are using the Common English Bible or another translation, IMMERSION BIBLE STUDIES will offer a refreshing plunge into God's Word, your life, and your life with God.

1.

Learning From the Past

Joshua 1–12

Claim Your Story

"Welcome to Lake Woebegone, where all the women are strong, all the men are good looking, and all the children are above average."[1] These familiar words by Garrison Keillor in his weekly radio show, *A Prairie Home Companion*, bring a smile—and maybe a chuckle—to his fans. In these words, we recognize our own penchant for romanticism and mythmaking when we reminiscence about family, community, and nation.

Our parents and grandparents hand down family stories of triumph during tough times—how we got through the Depression, how we participated in the Civil Rights Movement and the Vietnam War, how we managed when your dad lost his job. We tend to suppress the character flaws and missteps of those involved, although those flaws and missteps are integral to our identities. As a nation, we hand down stories of the first Thanksgiving with the Native Americans but suppress how the colonists later mistreated them. Nevertheless, that part of the story is as integral to our nation's identity as Thanksgiving itself.

Such accounts, while incomplete, give meaning to our past, help us to make sense of the present, and encourage hope for the future. They emerge from the way we string together certain events from our collective history to support our interpretation. For those of us who claim faith in God, how we do this reveals how we understand who God is and how God travels with us throughout life.

The Book of Joshua, written right before the Babylonians conquered the city and took the Jews into exile, reveals how the Israelites were interpreting their history with God. Joshua is a book about faith seeking understanding in the midst of impending doom—a spiritual discernment notebook written by the community. It is a collective reflection, but more than one voice is heard. Thus, Joshua doesn't conform to a set of comfortable faith lessons for today.

Speaking with more than one voice, the book invites us to see our lives in its reflection. It pushes us to consider what events and persons we exalt and/or suppress and for what purposes. How do we interpret how God has traveled with us?

Like Garrison Keillor's words about Lake Woebegone, the Book of Joshua helps us recognize our own mythmaking about our lives and faith in order to wring from it the truths that lie somewhere within—the truths that point us to God.

Enter the Bible Story

Introduction

The Book of Joshua was written a long time after the events it records. It's a faith document written for later Israelites who either were already in exile in Babylonia or were facing impending exile. They were trying to make sense of their present by looking back for something that could give them purpose, identity, meaning, and hope. Joshua tries to answer the questions, What did we do wrong? How can we be restored to fullness?

Joshua's text is not uniform but rather brings together various writings (stories, lists, exhortations, and so forth) that served different purposes and derived from diverse theological perspectives. While one overall narrator acts as the editor, the book has several storytellers with different perspectives of who God is and what God is doing.

Since the Israelites have lost their geographical identity and are living as strangers in another culture, the narrator reminds them of when God gave them the now-lost Promised Land. To discover where God is in their difficulties and why this is happening to them, the narrator recounts how their ancestors came to the land.

The different stories complicate the message of hope found in God's faithfulness to Israel. Counter stories interrupt the flow of divine conquest tales and challenge the traditional view of God's exclusivity to Israel and God's demand for ethnic purity as a pathway to a relationship with the Divine. Looking back to their glory days prompts the exile generation to consider their ongoing and ambivalent relationship with non-Israelites and ask, What type of allegiance and obedience does God truly desire? Is land and prosperity the reward of faithfulness? Is God accessible only to Jewish males, or does the Divine transcend these categories to have a covenantal relationship with women and non-Israelites as well? Was disposing of women and cattle truly what Yahweh desired?

These questions suggest that the Israelites were always a people of cultural and ethnic pluralism whose God blessed the faithfulness of both Israelites and non-Israelite men and women.

Joshua, Servant of God

Joshua, the main protagonist of this book, is unwavering in his fidelity to God, which was demonstrated in military excursions into the Promised Land. He obeys God's instructions even when they seem counterintuitive.

Moses changed Joshua's name from Hoshea, meaning "salvation," to Joshua, meaning "Yahweh is salvation" (Numbers 13:16). Hoshea alone cannot render salvation to the Israelites. However, as Joshua, he becomes Moses' successor in implementing Yahweh's salvation.

Like Moses, Joshua leads the Israelites to safely cross a river—this time the Jordan River—as God holds the waters at bay (Joshua 3). He sends out spies prior to taking the land (Chapter 2). He leads the Israelites to celebrate the Passover and renew their covenant with God (5:10-12). He comes face-to-face with a divine messenger who demands that he remove his sandals on holy ground. This vision prior to the fall of Jericho reinforces that God, not Joshua, is the one who saves Israel (5:13-15). "Yahweh is salvation" is the clear message of hope to remind the exile generation that God will not abandon them during the difficulty of captivity and landlessness.

Faithful Obedience Leads to Identity and Land

Salvation in the Book of Joshua is linked to obedience that is rewarded by the possession of land. In Chapter 1, God tells Joshua to be courageous, strong, and obedient as a sign of trust that God will give the land to Israel. The narrator puts forth what scholars call Deuteronomistic theology to make sense of the Israelites' life in exile. This theology holds that the Israelites' disobedience to God's law caused their defeat by the Babylonians. Therefore, the Book of Joshua reminds the Israelites of the time when they *were* faithful to God and when God was defeating their enemies and handing over land rights.

This theology prioritizes God's covenant to men such as Moses, Joshua, and the tribal leaders and seeks to demonstrate God's power and might. It is preoccupied with solidifying the identity of the Israelites in opposition to their neighbors by prohibiting intermarriages and cultural exchanges.

Therefore, the book condenses hundreds of years of settlement in Canaan into a brief timespan and offers a story of hope. It presses the importance of repentance and obedience by highlighting stories of harsh punishment for those who disobey God and reinforcing the importance of covenant renewal with God.

The dominant voice is that of the Deuteronomistic theologian, but counter voices reveal that the Israelites in exile did not find a simple faith formula sufficient for their complex reality. That reality included mixed-race kinships dating back to Abraham, Hagar, and Ishmael and Joseph and his half-Egyptian children.

The Taking of Jericho (Joshua 2–6)

The first counter story concerns the protection of Joshua's men on a reconnaissance mission to Jericho. The spies go to Rahab's house at the wall of Jericho, where the Common English Bible says they "bedded down" (2:1). The original Hebrew word has strong sexual overtones. The "spies are not above mixing business with pleasure"[2] and meet Rahab, a prostitute (notwithstanding the narrator's theology that forbids inter-mingling with foreigners or prostitutes). The Deuteronomistic theology is confronted with the fact that Rahab, a Canaanite, has been overwhelmed by God's acts and comes to believe in God's power. Therefore, she not only protects the spies from Jericho's king but also faces the king's men alone, misdirecting them to buy time for the spies' escape. Before the spies depart, she declares, "The LORD your God is God in heaven above and on earth below" (2:11). She also extracts a promise from them to keep her and her family safe. The spies instruct her to put a red scarf in her window so that her home will be passed over during the battle. The red scarf is reminiscent of the lamb's blood on the doorways of those in Egypt during the first Passover (Exodus 12:13). The greatest outsider—a foreigner, woman, and prostitute—and her family profess belief in God and are accepted into the Israelite community.

This story challenges the dominant theology that God has insiders and outsiders. It embraces the Deuteronomistic theology that faithfulness to God leads to identity and blessing. It hints that the identity God seeks is not ethnic or racial *but rather one of fidelity to right relationship with God and one another.*

The spies' confirmation to Joshua that Jericho is ready to be taken launches a series of divine acts that reinforce that God is keeping faith with the Israelites. God directs Joshua how to use the ark of the covenant to keep the Jordan River at bay and allow the people to cross unharmed. God then directs Joshua to have the Israelites memorialize God's faithfulness and this miracle with a pile of stones. This is followed with the miraculous fall of the Wall of Jericho and the destruction of its inhabitants (except Rahab and her family). Each event is punctuated with symbols from Israel's faith. The ark of the covenant is God's presence among them. Seven is a sacred number for ancient Hebrews and means "completion." The world was created in seven days and the Walls of Jericho came down in seven days. The Book of Joshua is saying, "Remember the mighty acts of God and remember your faithful obedience."

Israel Defeated at Ai (Joshua 7)

Obedience to God is rewarded, but how about disobedience? In the story of Achan, the unequivocal answer is that disobedience leads to death.

About the Scripture

(Un)Holy War

The Book of Joshua gives us a glimpse into the way ancient people thought about gods as beings who could be appeased by rituals and who were taken into battle to ensure triumph over their enemies.

The ancient theology, however contextualized, remains problematic within sacred texts where it can be and has been misappropriated by those who seek to justify their hate for a particular group. Indigenous peoples and their descendants who have been colonized and exploited may read Joshua and see a warrior God who seeks the destruction of some groups. They identify with the dispossession and violence inflicted on the Canaanites.

An example from my own Caribbean ancestry is the story my mother told me of the invasion of Cuba. The Taino indigenous chieftain, Hatuey, was burned alive at the stake at the hands of the Spanish conquistadores, and his people were disemboweled and torched. The Spanish priest, Bartolomé de la Casa, recorded the words of the chieftain to his people:

> These tyrants tell us they adore a God of peace and equality, yet they usurp our land and enslave us. They speak of an immortal soul and of eternal rewards and punishments. They rob us, seduce our women and violate our daughters. Unable to match us in valour, these cowards cover themselves in iron that our spears cannot pierce.[3]

Not only the conquistadores but also other exploiters have misused sacred texts as cover for their own agendas of economic gains and domination of others. The case of Hatuey in Cuba was replicated all over the globe as European nations colonized the New World, sometimes with the help of the Christian church. While the church, as in the case of Bartolomé de la Casa, advocated on behalf of the indigenous to stem the brutality of the conquistadors, it sometimes also eradicated indigenous faith and cultures, forcing Western ways upon them through "Christian" education. In the 19th and 20th centuries, Protestant missionary movements with good intentions fused the Gospel with forced separations of children from families for education, denying them the right to their indigenous language and culture.

In Joshua, the Deuteronomistic theologian's message that God does not abandon Israel and will restore it is accurate. However, God's blessing of restoration is not one of land and military power that coerces a false peace between the Canaanites and the Israelites. Instead, restoration includes right relationship with God *and* each other. God's promise to Abraham was to be a *blessing* to all the nations, not to eradicate them.

The Book of Joshua's holy wars are indeed unholy. Its presence in our sacred texts is a reminder of how we must be awake to our own tendencies to distort God's salvation for our own purposes. They bear witness of how powerfully human desires for control and wealth work against God's inclination for justice.

God instructed the Israelites to not keep any spoils of their pillage of Jericho. Thus, when Achan keeps some of the goods, God's wrath is poured out. Joshua understands that Achan's individual act has jeopardized the entire people. Achan's confession and punishment, therefore, absolves Israel. God demands that his entire clan share Achan's punishment, and they are all stoned to death. The narrator is asserting that the reason for Israel's exile is its disobedience to God.

There is another way to read the story of Achan. This is the second counter voice to the Deuteronomistic theology. Danna Fewell, an Old Testament scholar, notes, "[Achan] is the direct opposite of Rahab. Whereas Rahab, a Canaanite woman, saves her whole family, Achan, an Israelite man, is instrumental in destroying his."[4] Faithfulness to God in Rahab's case is not tied to culture or ethnicity. Rather, Rahab's faithfulness is wedded to reverence for God.

God Protects the Gibeonites (Joshua 9)

Another counter story concerns Gibeonites who use trickery to obtain a promise of protection from Joshua and the tribal leaders. The Gibeonites hid their identity as Canaanites by pretending to be bedraggled nomads from afar who stumbled upon the military conflict. They sought protection and offered themselves as servants in exchange.

God indirectly sanctions the Gibeonites' decision to live among the Israelites through the oath Joshua swore on God's name. Even after discovering the deception, Joshua could not disavow the Gibeonites because doing so would be to disrespect God. Thus, Joshua protected the Gibeonites by making them servants to the Israelites. This story explains how it is that the Gibeonites came to live among the Israelites as servants well into the time when the Joshua narrative was written.

The Final Miracle (Joshua 10–11)

The miracle of when the "sun stood still" (10:13) tells of Joshua's military cunning that strategically leads Canaanite forces into the blinding sun as God sends lethal hailstones upon them. While God's might stands far above the power of the Canaanite gods, the fact that Joshua, not God, is the one to command the sun to stand still, underscores his divine anointment to take the land.

This colorful story of a miracle backing up military plans is followed in Chapter 11 by a recap of the conquest of the rest of the territory and the assassination of the remaining Canaanite kings. Chapter 11 ends with the statement, "So Joshua took the whole land, exactly as the LORD had promised Moses. Joshua gave it as a legacy to Israel according to their tribal shares. Then the land had a rest from war" (verse 23). The glory-days story of how God kept the promise of land and prosperity to an obedient Israel comes to an end.

Live the Story

We can identify with the desire and hope for a do-over when we make a mess of things. The Book of Joshua points to God's boundless love for the Israelites, and through them, to us. With the retelling of history, God gives the Israelites an opportunity for a do-over.

Second chances are opportunities to understand who God is and to see ourselves with new eyes. This opportunity, however, requires courage to look at uncomfortable truths and to turn away (repent) from the wrongs they show us. Only then can we experience transformation. Unfortunately, our human, sinful tendency is to gloss over, or worse, rewrite the uncomfortable truths and create rigid, exclusionary rules of order. Instead, we should strive to release ourselves into God's redemptive love to transform our mistakes and misjudgments.

In Joshua, we see how the Israelites fell into this same tendency toward rigidity and away from God's redemptive and liberating love. It retells the Israelites' history with a strong dose of judgment against their feeble faith in God and against anyone who didn't live under prescribed faith rules. The dominant voice wants to remember Israel's history of possessing the land by covering up their historical relationships with the Canaanites. Yet, by the grace of God, the counter-voice stories that disrupt this dominant-voice tendency manage to live within it and survive across centuries. They allow us to consider the questions, Is God's faithfulness for an exclusive group? How does God reveal God's self to humanity? Can those who do not know any teachings of God experience God?

We continue to ponder these important questions as we walk by faith with God. Yet, one thing that the Israelites settled for us is this: the greatness of their God is found in the power of God's love for all, and God's love and presence are not bounded by culture or land.

Similar to the dominant narrator's tendency to overlook certain aspects of Israel's history in Joshua, we are tempted to look away from our flaws and personal history and choose to hide the shame of abuse or violence in families or communities. Second chances and do-overs from broken relationships with others, from addictions, from immaturity, and from institutional abuses offer us the opportunity to find God's redeeming work within the difficulties, as well as clarity of mind to let go of hurtful patterns. (For example, collectively, we have uncovered the violence done to African Americans and Native Americans, which has resulted in healing for some.) If we choose to gloss over these flaws and abuses, we keep ourselves bound to the power of the violence. The moment when we expose them is when we are able to redirect our lives and gain a new vision of what God intends for us.

Will we take God's gift of a second chance to unclench our fists and open our hands to one another? Will we trust God's unfathomable love to lead to new imaginations for life together?

---

[1] From *http://prairiehome.publicradio.org/about/podcast/*.
[2] From *Joshua in The Women's Bible Commentary*, by Danna Nolan Fewell; edited by Carol A. Newsom and Sharon H. Ringe (Westminster John Knox Press, 1998); page 66.
[3] From *http://www.onaway.org/indig/taino2.htm*.
[4] From *Joshua* (Fewell); page 64.

2.

Expanded Horizons and a Renewed Covenant

Joshua 13–24

Claim Your Story

I remember being awestruck by the grandeur of the Basilica of St. Peter in Vatican City and the Al-Aqsa Mosque in Jerusalem when I traveled to both as a college student. Both houses of worship are immense and beautiful. The Basilica, built in the fourth century at the site of St. Peter's grave, is full of great works of art by Michelangelo, including the *Pieta* and the Sistine Chapel. Its frescoes, marble, and gold inspire reverence. The Al-Aqsa Mosque with its open courtyards peppered with flora of various types, calligraphy art, mosaics, and majestic columns evoke a different type of reverence. Built about 1,300 years ago, the mosque has 35 acres and 11 gates and sits on Temple Mount where the shrine of the Dome of the Rock (a golden splendor that is the hallmark of Jerusalem's landscape) was erected to mark the spot where the prophet Mohammed was lifted into the Seven Heavens.[1]

The impulse to commemorate our experience of the Divine with the best sacred spaces that our minds, hearts, and hands can create is part of our human history. These spaces allow us to gather to share our sacred stories, remember God's faithfulness, and renew our commitment to and faith in God.

The second half of the Book of Joshua begins with a description of how the land was divided among the tribes that comprised Israel. It ends with the account of the Israelites' renewed commitment to God, and it is in these final chapters that we hear the essential message of this second half. There we read how Joshua exhorted the Israelites to recommit themselves to God in response to God's faithfulness. They solemnized their vow to Yahweh and created a sacred space within their sanctuary to bear witness to the generations that would follow (24:26-27). Prior to that, the Israelite tribes living on the east side of the Jordan River built a great altar they called a "witness" to bear testimony that "the Lord is God" (22:10-34). They are sacred spaces because they remind the Israelites that God's faithfulness to love and redeem extends to all humanity.

Today we also build sacred spaces and create sacred rituals to honor God, spaces where we can share stories, remember God's faithfulness, and renew our faith and commitment to follow God. As it was for the Israelites, some of our sacred spaces are places of great horror and pain—such as the September 11, 2001 memorial in New York City. Others are grand cathedrals such as Westminster Abbey and artful large and small houses of worship built to honor and revere God. Others are not physical spaces but practices of peace, unity, and blessing. The last chapters of the Book of Joshua remind us that the power of sacred spaces—where we gather as God's children, remember God's faithfulness, and renew our faith—is found in how they help us to bear witness to God's love and justice.

What are the sacred places where you have encountered God's transformation? Has it been a mission trip? your local congregation? an encounter with someone? How do these sacred places help you spread God's hope for those who are hurting and feel excluded in your neighborhood—the poor, elderly, single moms, gay and lesbian individuals, Muslim families, or immigrants?

Enter the Bible Story

Expanded Horizons of Equity: The Accepted Claims of Daughters

Reading Chapters 13–21 in Joshua can be tedious. The narrator has pieced together lists from various sources to create a central record so the Israelites can remember how the land was divided among the twelve tribes and their descendants. The narrator makes it clear that the land was apportioned according to God's instructions and that Joshua and the priest Eleazar are doing God's bidding. In addition to recording who inherits which territory, the narrator delivers a secondary, and probably unintended, message. That secondary message is found in the absence of female names as inheritors in favor of male heads of households. That absence reveals that the marginalization of women from economic and social power was understood as sanctioned by God.

Why is this exhaustive account so important? For one reason, the detailed lists with household names show that God is faithful to fulfill the promises made in the covenant with Abraham (Genesis 15:1-7) and later with the Israelites under Moses (Exodus 19:5-8; Leviticus 20:24). The lists remind those who read them of God's faithfulness to each tribe.

The other reason these detailed lists are important is to help re-establish Israel as a nation after the exile (remember from Session One that Joshua was written long after the events it records). After being in exile for so many years, the later generations of Israelites needed both a reminder that God had given the land to them and a document to guide how the land was to be reoccupied. Thus, the Book of Joshua offers a record of the original distribution of the territories as that guide.

As in the first 12 chapters, the second half of Joshua includes disruptions to the Deuteronomistic narrator's central faith message. In this second half, the primary faith message is that God makes covenants with male Israelite tribal leaders, and that God's fidelity is demonstrated by making them the sole inheritors of the Promised Land. But the power of the dominant theological viewpoint continues to be challenged by included stories that disrupt the otherwise tidy narrative. These stories, while small, are strong in their confrontation of the religious and social norms assumed by the main narrator. They make different claims about the nature of Yahweh's blessings and who is entitled to receive them.

First, we have the story of Caleb, who is given land in reward for his loyalty to Moses and obedience to God (Numbers 14:24; Joshua 15:13-19). God is responding to Caleb's faithfulness and is not bound by Caleb's lack of a tribal role. The story gets more interesting when Caleb's daughter, Achsah, approaches her father after he bequeaths her husband a tract of land from his territory. Achsah realizes that the land needs a source of water to make it useful and life-giving. Therefore, she boldly asks her father for a complete inheritance, including a water source, which Caleb gives her. Achsah's own words to her father stand strong within the text and are followed by the gift of water, revealing the dignity of her claim.

Another disruption is Zelophehad's daughters' claim directly to Joshua for an inheritance of land (17:3-6). Mahlah, Noah, Hoglah, Milcah, and Tirzah's words stand out strongly in the text as a challenge to the exclusive rights of male household leaders. They point out that their household of women and children has been faithful to God's covenant and to Joshua's leadership. The tragic death of their father and their lack of brothers or uncles of age did not change the household's loyalty. These sisters teach Joshua that God's faithfulness extends to them too, for they have been faithful just as the male heads of households and tribes have been faithful. Therefore, they believe that God will not deny them their due inheritance of land.

Joshua agreed, and he gave the women and their household their rightful inheritance. Since the text has established that Joshua and Eleazar are Yahweh's servants, it is, in fact, Yahweh who has given Zelophehad's daughters the land. This story exposes the injustice of a patriarchal system that leaves women impoverished and challenges the cultural viewpoint that women could not inherit land. The daughters' faithfulness empowered them to lay claim on God's faithfulness as preached by Joshua and Eleazar. The text thus dismantles the sociopolitical and religious norms that guided life in those times. It speaks to the everyday life of women in exile whose rightful claims of land upon return to their homeland were likely to be denied.

Expanded Horizons of Divine Justice: The Cities of Refuge

Another disruption is found in Chapter 20 when the Lord commands that three cities—Kedesh, Shechem, and Hebron—be set apart as cities of refuge. The dominant Deuteronomistic theology taught that the land was completely handed over to the Israelites and that the Canaanites were expelled handily so as to create a populace that was exclusively Israelite.

In this brief section, however, the Lord sets up sanctuaries for Israelites *and immigrants residing among them* so that they may be protected from murderous vengeance if they accidentally killed someone (20:9). This provision for immigrants shows that the divine love of justice and compassion is present within an otherwise vengeful societal ethic, and it includes non-Israelites. This story's presence in the text points to an alternative view of God as the giver of a new ethic for how humans were to relate to each other.

Losing Sight of God's Expanded Horizons: When Fear Rules the Practice of Religion

Chapter 22 tells of an immense altar built by the Reubenites, Gadites, and half the tribe of Manasseh (who lived in separate territory from the other half of their tribe [see 12:6 and 17:2]). While nine-and-a-half tribes settled west of the Jordan River, these two-and-a-half tribes were given territory on the east side. In response to this gift of land, these tribes built a large altar to God. The Israelites on the west side of the Jordan heard about this and worried that this unusually large altar was a *challenge* to God instead of an *honor* to God. They worried that these eastern tribes had jeopardized them all by dishonoring the Lord. For this reason, they prepared to fight their Israelite kin to the death if necessary. But first, they sent a delegation to the eastern group, led by Eleazar. The eastern tribes told the delegation that they had built the altar because they feared that future generations on their side of the river would one day question their inclusion as God's people. The enormous altar was to forestall that and be a testimony of their gratitude to God. Hearing this, the delegation from the western tribes was satisfied that all was well, and harmony among the tribes on both sides of the Jordan River was restored.

The Israelites' conflict over the great altar's purpose resonates with our conflicts over the purposes of the structures we build. We are wary of each other's motives. In the 12th century, Francis of Assisi challenged the opulence and gold found in the Christian cathedrals and set up congregations in the forests where the poor lived. The labor of love from our hands that creates great art in honor of God is a worthy thing. It is an act of great devotion and reverence. The real question is whether we become so bound by the buildings and their trappings that we lose sight of what is important to God. Are the buildings and our rituals means of grace that lead us to God? The prophets Isaiah (58:1-14) and Micah (6:6-8) remind the Israelites that leaving God behind can happen even when they continue to make offerings and participate in worship. They leave God behind when they fail to be in relationships of compassion with one another.

The Renewal of the Covenant with God

Chapter 24 ends the Book of Joshua with a speech where Joshua recounts God's miraculous works on behalf of the Israelites. He exhorts them to pledge their allegiance to Yahweh and to avoid foreign gods, telling them that to do otherwise would bring God's judgment and destruction upon them. In response, the Israelites wholeheartedly renew their covenant with God and promise complete fidelity.

This is a fitting ending to a story written for Israelites who have experienced defeat at the hands of the Babylonians. The way to restoration was to gather together, remember their collective stories of God's faithfulness, and renew their faith.

The Book of Joshua exposes the faith crisis experienced by the later people of Israel as they sought to make sense of their social and economic situation at the time of the Babylonian exile. The faith crisis is revealed in two perspectives: the text's dominant view and the disruptions of this view also contained in the text.

The dominant view expressed in the text reminded the Israelites of God's faithfulness and urged them to renew their faith. It did so by reconstructing a history that favored Israel as God's chosen people as the end in and of itself instead of as God's people chosen to be a blessing to all the nations.

The disruptions throughout the Book of Joshua reveal the forces that worked against the total rewriting of the Israelite history. First, they reveal that eradication of the Canaanites from the land did not happen and that God does not always sanction it. Instead, Canaanites were capable of responding to God's mighty acts with courageous acts of kindness and justice. Second, the reward of land was not an exclusive right of male Israelites; it extended to Canaanites and women too. Third, the entire dispute about whether the large altar built by the eastern tribes was to honor Yahweh exposes how religion and national security were sometimes colluding.

About the Scripture

Jesus and the New Covenant

A covenant is a binding agreement between parties. In Joshua 23:16, Joshua warns the Israelites not to violate the "covenant of the LORD." In the next chapter, he calls on the people to serve God faithfully (which was how they were to keep their side of the covenant). Finally, after the people agreed to serve God faithfully, Joshua, representing the Lord, made a fresh covenant with them (24:25).

Jesus offers a new covenant that is summed up in what he identifies as the two greatest commandments (Matthew 22:37-40). In establishing the special meal we call the Lord's Supper, Jesus "took a cup, gave thanks, and gave it to them, saying, 'Drink from this, all of you. This is my blood of the covenant, which is poured out for many so that their sins may be forgiven'" (Matthew 26:27-28).

Sacred spaces and sacred rituals are those that exist within Jesus' new covenant of relationships of grace with God and our sisters and brothers across race, culture, and class. His covenant leads us to a shared love full of forgiveness, hope, and life everlasting.

The disruptions in the text also offer some emerging faith understandings of God's nature that pushed against the picture of God as a warrior handing over the Promised Land to the Israelites and decreeing total destruction of the peoples already there. God cares for both the Israelites and the Canaanites who call upon his name. God blesses Hagar, Ishmael, Joseph's half-Egyptian children, and their descendents, recognizing the kinship between them and all the tribes of Israel. God sees women as human beings capable of courage, intelligence, and great acts of faith and eligible to inherit land. God also demands refuge and justice for all people when he establishes the cities of refuge.

The Book of Joshua exposes the danger of making God in the image of our own agendas, including agendas that seek to justify excluding or oppressing those who are different from us. Our religious history of the Inquisition and the continuing plight of Native Americans and colonized populations all over the globe are evidence of the evil that can transpire when we project our agendas on the Divine. Today, we must ask ourselves if we live within the covenant with God to be a blessing to all. Who do we include? exclude? Have we built churches ("a great altar") to boast and separate ourselves from others, or have we built them as "mixed-use real estate"—a sacred space—by which to show our gratitude to a God of hope for all?

Live the Story

The Book of Joshua reminds us that the imminent danger of crafting God to fit our agendas lurks in every generation. Today, our world has religious radicals from the three major world religions—Islam, Judaism, and Christianity—who misuse sacred texts as justification for violence against each other.

The Israelites who were trying to rebuild their community had a choice to repeat past mistakes or to recast how they understood God's will. They knew that they were not one pure race and that their land had not been acquired in a short period of conquest. Rather, the land had been settled over hundreds of years through a combination of intermarriages and battles. Unfortunately, their faith language designated some of their neighbors as outside of legal protection. That language enforced a political ethic that ignored their rich faith legacy of God's blessing to Abraham, Hagar, and Ishmael, and to Joseph and his Egyptian-Hebrew biracial children alongside of Sarah and Isaac. They struggled to make room for social and religious acceptance of the Canaanites living among the Israelites (either separately or through intermarriages).

In our lives, we too rewrite our own stories—individual, faith community, and national—as a spiritual practice to discern what God is teaching us through difficult times. We also have a choice to repeat our mistakes or to recast how we understand God's desire for us. Will we begin modern

Inquisitions against different sets of people? Will we strive against other faiths for the upper hand as Christians did against each other during the Reformation?

Since September 11, 2001, many cities have formed interfaith programs to allow Christian, Muslim, and Jewish congregations to join in a witness for peace. In Dallas, Texas, where I live, there are several informal groups and a nonprofit organization called Thanks-Giving Square that bring together all religions for dialogue. Interfaith groups like these have promoted peace in cities across our great nation and have allowed honest relationships of respect and compassion to be forged. They become, in effect, sacred spaces.

Nevertheless, our cities have also been sites of arson against mosques and Jewish synagogues. We have radical fundamental Christian groups who want to publicly burn the Qur'an and who picket soldiers' funerals because of the acceptance of homosexuals in society. We also have had a rise of attacks against African-American and Latino/a citizens by rogue groups who strive for white supremacy. One US company was heavily pressured to drop its sponsorship of a new reality TV show about Muslim-Americans. We also live in a time when some denominations use faith language to advance judgment against gay, lesbian, bisexual, or transgendered people. In some places, faith and religion are still being co-opted for sociopolitical reasons. Nevertheless, God moves toward us over and over again with a love that is known by its justice for all.

How do the stories from Joshua reveal what you fear? What areas of your life need to be expanded by God's love? Imagine the life together that God's love for all humanity desires. What can you do, with God's help, to make this life a sacred space?

---

[1] From *http://www.atlastours.net/holyland/al_aqsa_mosque.html.*

3.

How Does God Bless Us?

Judges 1–9

Claim Your Story

In my youth, my Protestant Latino/a church held annual revivals—*campañas*. One year, our guest evangelist was a middle-aged former gang member. Raised in New York City, his family was Puerto Rican. His powerful *testimonio* was of transformation by God's love that redeemed him from the abyss of bad decisions, violence, drugs, and prison. He had strayed far from God, but God's love delivered him and led him into a Christian ministry to gang members. Our congregation was moved by his story and by the assurance that when we accept God's faithful love, we are delivered from our bad decisions and our lives are blessed.

Life, however, is complicated, and we often are buffeted by difficulties in spite of accepting God's love. We experience tragic accidents, terminal illnesses, natural disasters, violence, economic downturns, and political forces that lead to war. We sometimes experience these catastrophes even when we are faithfully obedient to God. When this occurs, we may ask, Where is God? We are forced to consider whether accepting God's love really means that our lives will be blessed and that we will be delivered from bad decisions.

Thus, we ask different questions: How does God faithfully love and bless us? Does our faithlessness result in these catastrophes as God's punishment? How does God transform life? What do we do about our faith in God when religion becomes a tool for oppression?

These are the questions that the Book of Judges puts forth, not only for the ancient Israelites but also for us.

Enter the Bible Story

Introduction

It is difficult to read the Book of Judges without cringing because some passages portray God ordering land grabs and genocide. Native Americans and others whose history is one of conquest and colonization sometimes find the God presented in Judges difficult to access. It is particularly difficult for women to read Judges' stories of abuse against women, stories that range from domestic violence and gang rape to even female sacrifice. These stories are horrifying and cannot be explained away.

One purpose of Judges seems to be to justify Israel's need to establish a monarchy with centralized military power. It makes the case that the individual Israelite tribes were too weak to possess Canaan singly, but together they would be a formidable power. Judges also preaches that their lack of faithfulness to Yahweh led to their eventual defeat.

Judges was written many years after the stories in Judges occurred. Its audience was Jews who found themselves without a state of their own after the fall of Judah to the Babylonians. Therefore, the book deals with this community's crisis of faith. It reminds them that their ancestors' unfaithfulness to God and lack of unity as tribes allowed them to be overpowered by the Canaanites. It aims to move these later Jews to repentance and renewal of the covenant with Yahweh.

Judges interprets God's covenant with Abraham and Moses in a particular theological perspective of power, land, and conquest. Centralization of power and acquisition of land requires the removal of any ethical or relational sympathies toward non-Israelites and of any inheritance claims to land by non-Israelites. Judges uses religious language to justify genocide and conquest. It mirrors ancient times when deities were taken into battle and were considered the lead warriors defending their people.

In the 21st century, we benefit from the whole Bible, which shows us that a warrior God whose strength is proven by military victories and land acquisition is an inadequate image of Yahweh. We understand Yahweh's covenant in light of justice and compassion found in the prophets and in the higher ethic of radical love for one another, including our enemies, found in Jesus' message. While the Judges' message to the Jews that God is faithful and will never abandon them rings true, the *form* of that faithfulness needs to be viewed in the broader context of the whole Bible. By itself, the Book of Judges gives us a snapshot of how a well-intentioned but incomplete revelation of God's purpose and nature can allow evil to flourish at the hands of religion. This snapshot also shows that the deficiencies of a patriarchal society can prove deadly. In its central message of God's fidelity and in its uncomfortable portrayal of the evil that flourishes, the Book of Judges offers important ethical and faith insights relevant to our lives today.

The Deuteronomistic Theologian as Narrator

Judges makes a case for Israel to establish a monarchy to bring order and centralize power under Yahweh's covenant. This narrative contrasts sharply with the Book of Joshua's description of God handing over the land to the Israelites over a relatively short period. It provides a more realistic account of how the Israelites settled the Canaanite land and why they were unable to fully possess it. At the same time, it still falls within the Deuteronomistic viewpoint, explaining that Israel's fate is due to its apostasy from the true worship of God.

Judges explains the difficulty ancient Israel had in taking ownership of the land as follows: "As a test for Israel, to see whether they would carefully walk in the LORD's ways just as their ancestors had done, the LORD left these nations instead of driving them out immediately or handing them over to Joshua" (2:22-23). This sets up a cause-and-effect theology to answer the difficult questions of later Israel's new landlessness and defeat. It also assumes that the Israelites' interpretation of God's promise to Abraham and Moses is indisputable, that God's promise of a vast nation was a literal monarchy with plenty of real estate, wealth, and military power. Israelites held onto this understanding through generations of slavery and oppression, and it reflects the ancient understanding and use of deities in society.

The Deuteronomistic narrator situates the stories of Judges in a literary pattern to make the case in favor of a divinely appointed monarch and to remind Israel that God has not forgotten them, in spite of their fickleness. The pattern is that "Israel does evil in Yahweh's sight; Yahweh gives the people into the hand of oppressors; Israel cries to Yahweh; Yahweh raises up a deliverer; the deliverer defeats the oppressor; the people are faithful while the deliverer is alive and the land has rest."[1]

Othniel (3:7-11) is the first model judge who fits this pattern, and Ehud (3:12-30) is the next. After God sends each of these deliverers, the narrator reports that Israel enjoys a time of peace and prosperity. Following the pattern, Israel eventually disobeys God, and the cycle begins again.

The early story in Chapter 3 of how Ehud murders the fat Moabite king, Eglon, reads like a modern black comedy. This same is true for Sisera's death in Chapter 4. The thirst for Canaanite blood in these two early stories is so vivid that it becomes comical in the darkest sense; they are too horrible to hold as a straight drama, and the reader releases an uncomfortable laugh. A modern example of this is the film *Pulp Fiction*, whose characters' distorted attempts to form a code of ethics within the context of a wholly immoral life is so dark that the most violent scenes evoke pain mixed with laughter, a coping device. This is what happens in Judges. In Deborah's song (5:2-31), the lyrics rejoice in Sisera's and his mother's defeat with no hint of remorse for the carnage and the acceptance of rape as soldiers' rewards. These early stories foreshadow the descent into blood, gore, and ruthlessness in subsequent tales. Soon, we cannot distinguish the actions of the Canaanites from those of the Israelites, as both are equally heinous.

As each story becomes more offensive than the last, the narrator changes his literary pattern for a new one. In Chapters 17–21, a pattern emerges: "In those days there was no king in Israel; each person did what they thought to be right" (17:6; 21:25; see also 18:1; 19:1). The new pattern clearly signals that Israel's tribal leadership is ineffective and that a monarch is the answer.

Deborah, Barak, Jael, and Sisera (Judges 4–5)

Chapter 4 introduces Deborah as a prophet and judge of Israel from whom the people seek advice. The narrator offers little about her private life except that, as an aside, she is married to Lappidoth. Her identity is her public role as prophet, leader, and "mother" in Israel (4:4; 5:7). In that role, she summons

Barak and gives him a message from the Lord. That he responds readily to her summons lets the reader know that she is respected. Still, Barak seems to question her authority when he doesn't completely trust the prophecy she gives him. It is surprising to have a woman receive a direct word from the Lord within what is otherwise a male-centered narrative.

Why do we have a story of a strong woman in Judges? Barak fits the Deuteronomistic understanding of men as God's chosen leaders, and so his lack of trust in Deborah is consistent with the socioreligious norms. Therefore, Barak is a sympathetic character when he questions Deborah's authority as a prophet. Barak will only agree to do the Lord's bidding of conquering Sisera, the Canaanite general, if Deborah accompanies him in battle. Deborah agrees but gives him a prophecy that is shaming to a man in a patriarchal society. She tells him that his lack of confidence in her prophecy (and thereby his lack of trust in the Lord) means that the ultimate victory over Sisera will be a woman's doing and not his.

Of course, the reader and perhaps Barak immediately think she is speaking of herself. This is reinforced by the fact that while Barak is in command of the military theater, Deborah directs his actions. It is Yahweh's prophecy to Deborah and Yahweh's direct action of throwing Sisera's men into a panic that make it possible for Barak and his soldiers to overpower Sisera's army and eventually the Canaanite king, Jabin.

True to Deborah's prophecy, Barak does not kill Sisera, who escapes on foot. Sisera makes it to what should be a safe haven for him, the encampment of Kenites who are neutral in the wars between the Canaanites and the Israelites. The Kenites are itinerant metal workers who make weapons for both sides to maintain neutrality. Sisera arrives at the tent of Heber, whose wife, Jael, greets him and offers him milk and rest. As he rests, Jael makes an autonomous decision to drive a stake through his temple, killing him instantly. The most unexpected and unlikely person—a woman and an artisan—accomplishes Sisera's defeat.

The story has now introduced us to a second woman of strength, Jael, who enjoys God's blessing. She perceives that Sisera's arrival on foot meant that the Israelites have defeated the Canaanites. She could not refuse hospitality to an armed general, but she knows aiding him jeopardizes the neutrality of her people. She quickly surmises that to protect her tribe from the victors' wrath, she must show solidarity with the Israelites. Thus, she literally takes matters into her own hands. The calculating and bloody murder of the sleeping Sisera (after granting him refuge) assaults readers' sensibilities. However, because she joined Yahweh in the defeat of the Canaanites, Jael is extolled in Deborah's song, and her murderous act is embellished (5:24-27).

Deborah and Jael are powerful women. Deborah, the prophet and judge, receives revelations from God and demonstrates courage and military prowess. Jael, an otherwise unknown wife who belongs to a tribe that tries to live under the radar, emerges as one of Israel's most blessed (5:24). The narrator of Judges is preaching that God is birthing a new nation, protecting his chosen people, and nurturing a new way of life by handing the Israelites the land and defeating the Canaanites. Jael and Deborah, Israel's "mother," act as agents of liberation and join Yahweh in acts that birth, protect, and nurture Israel.

About the Scripture

Deborah's Song

This song (Judges 5:2-31) is one of the oldest texts found in the Old Testament, dating back to the 12th century B.C., and it is in a literary form that was also used by the ancient Egyptians and Assyrians. The song celebrates the defeat of the Canaanites and extols Deborah and Jael for their courage and faithfulness. Yahweh is clearly the warrior God in charge of this holy battle.

The song is an example of early Hebrew poetry. Scholar P.C. Craigie wrote about the similarities between the Song of Deborah and the earlier Assyrian Tukulti-Ninurta Epic.[2] The purpose of both is to retell a military triumph within the language of faith to affirm the strength and power of the deity and justify human actions.

In ancient times, battles were a test of not only a nation's strength but also the strength of the nation's gods. Prayers before and during the battle were important, and prophets often accompanied the soldiers to give them spiritual strength before meeting their enemies. The poems show how ancient peoples did not separate faith from their everyday lives, including politics and economics. Economics often meant putting together alliances of various tribes under one ruler to capture as much fertile land as possible. This helps explain the presence of Deborah's song in the Book of Judges.

"Lord, Give Me a Sign—Again and Again and Again…and Maybe…"
(Judges 6–8)

Gideon's story falls nicely within Judges' literary pattern. After Deborah's song, the text reads, "And the land was peaceful for forty years. The Israelites did things that the LORD saw as evil, and the LORD handed them over to the Midianites for seven years" (5:31–6:1). Yahweh once again offers a deliverer, only this time the leader is a reluctant, faithless warrior—Gideon. Gideon reminds us of Moses with his doubts and questions (Exodus 3–4), but unlike Moses, he never gains faith. When the Lord's messenger speaks to him, Gideon protests that he is an insignificant person from the weakest tribe, and he insists on a test before he will take the message seriously.

Gideon asks a cynical question: Where has the powerful Yahweh been for the past seven years while they [his people] suffered poverty and fear at the hands of the Midianites? In response, the divine messenger asks Gideon to dethrone Baal from his father's altar. Gideon does not make the connection, however, that Israel's faithlessness to God is the cause of their suffering at the hand of the Midianites. Yet it is very clear in the story that when the Israelites walk away from God, they pay a price in suffering. Therefore, the first step toward restoration and deliverance is to reestablish the worship of Yahweh.

Gideon is an interesting choice for a leader because even when he asks for sign after sign from God and God generously indulges him, he remains unchanged. In the miraculous victory over Midian with just 300 men (a sign of God's presence and deliverance), Gideon does not praise Yahweh. The story is filled with vengeful triumph. The decapitated heads of the Midianite soldiers Oreb and Zeeb are brought to Gideon. He takes revenge against the people of Succoth and Penuel for having denied his army provisions. Gideon is caught up in the power of triumph and uses it with glee against anyone who goes against him.

Gideon's character, weak from the start, is now sinking fast and will sink further. He seems to be doing God's bidding only because his demands for signs are being met, leaving him no excuses to delay. He remains cynical, unable to reflect on the battlefield miracles and displays no loyalty to God.

Instead, he seems to gloat with power and takes nasty revenge on fellow Israelites for minor slights (8:4-17). His character has fallen into cynicism and self-importance.

Gideon's final descent is revealed in his refusal to become the Israelites' leader, a position from which he could steer the tribes back toward faithfulness to Yahweh. Instead, he requests and receives gold from the people, using it to make a breastplate with an idol on it (*ephod*). Gideon does not wait several years to commit idolatry. He walks away from Yahweh immediately after leaving his role as Israel's deliverer.

Gideon personifies the Israelites' spiritual blindness and idolatry in the years after Moses and Joshua. In spite of God's repeated deliverance, Israel, like Gideon, remains unchanged. Israel, like Gideon, takes God's gift of power and deliverance without any sense of gratitude or reverence for God. The Israelites have an opportunity to see their own reflection in Gideon's actions and lack of faith.

The first eight chapters of Judges lead us to a spiritual dead end. The message that God can choose one ethnic group or nation over another for blessing is inadequate. It reduces the Divine to human acts of foolishness fueled by the desire to conquer and dominate others. Reading these ancient stories against the backdrop of sacred texts that follow it, we see that this picture of God is distorted. The Canaanites and the Israelites are spiritually empty. That emptiness leads to the false premise that God's blessing is a scarce commodity. Since it is scarce, it has to be hoarded and protected by a select few for a select few. As a result, both the Israelites and the Canaanites sink into an abyss of unspeakable violence.

Live the Story

The Book of Judges depicts a shortsighted understanding of God's blessing as consisting of land, prosperity, and peace. The text shows that whenever a leader overpowers the oppressors, Israel has peace for a limited time. Could it be that the Israelites chose to bend the covenant and God's promise of blessing to fit their human desire for nation building and military power? As the text reveals, peace cannot be sustained through violent power grabbing. In this book, people are destroyed in the name of holy war, but the reward is nothing but a further descent into inhumanity.

Judges makes us examine the precept that if we are good, God will bless us with prosperity, but if we have been unfaithful, we will experience tragedy. Life has many tragedies that just happen and are inexplicable. Life also has many tragedies that are completely avoidable and are constructed for the sake of the few who choose to use power over others. Does that mean that God's power is not palpable? No! God's presence is transformative, just as Jesus' presence was transformative to the people of Galilee. God is present in our faithfulness during life's tragedies and in our resistance to institutionally created problems. Didn't God show that his love is stronger than death in the resurrection of Jesus?

How is God blessing you? What needs to be transformed in your life? In what ways are you bringing this need before God?

[1] From *Judges* in *The Women's Bible Commentary*, by Danna Nolan Fewell; edited by Carol A. Newsom and Sharon H. Ringe (Westminster John Knox Press, 1998); page 67.
[2] From "The Song of Deborah and the Epic of Tikulti-Ninurta" in *Journal of Biblical Literature*, by P.C. Craigie (1969); pages 253-265.

4.

Standing Against Oppression

Judges 10–21

Claim Your Story

As a 22-year-old seminarian, I ministered to 18-year-old brides from Puerto Rico who had followed their new husbands, first-time Army recruits, to a US Army base. Talking with them, I unexpectedly discovered that they experienced domestic violence. My Bible studies and conversations with the women were filled by their pressing question, If marriage is God ordained, is it not a sin for me to leave my husband, even if he is beating the children and me? In other words, how do I keep God's rules and literally *live*?

Sometimes our religious teachings come up short in the face of evil and tragedy, especially if our teachings are bound to denominational rules instead of God's life-giving redemption. I offered the women this thought: "God is love and offers love and life to you and all humanity. God's will is not suffering or an untimely death and cruelty." This placed the question of marital covenant alongside God's desire for abundant life and God's love for all. The marital covenant had already been breached by the violence. The difficulty was that the religious denominations (there were various represented) taught that women were to be subject to their husbands and their husbands to God. As a Latino/a fellowship, this view reinforced the cultural machismo that gave men the power over money that kept women trapped. It also dispensed extraordinary forgiveness to men for their violent behavior and very little to women for their errors. Since, in their minds, God was male, the women could not imagine themselves as wholly created in God's image and therefore beloved. God was not their liberator but their captor.

Years later when I volunteered in a domestic violence shelter, I had the same conversations with middle-class Caucasian women. Although they had the courage to leave their husbands, they struggled with guilt based on the same religious teaching and chose to return to their batterers to keep from "sinning."

Faith in God helps us navigate through many ethical decisions, but difficulty comes when our religious institutions and their teachings contradict the nature of God. In the final chapters of Judges, the Israelites lose complete sight of God and God's teachings. People make moral and ethical decisions without a moral compass. When God is evoked, God does not respond, but the Israelites do not notice; they simply continue to do as they see right and ascribe it to God. In this frightful second half of Judges, we are confronted with our inclination to do the same.

Enter the Bible Story

Descent into Moral Chaos: The Price of a Daughter (Judges 11:1–12:7)

Judges shocks us when the Israelites' departure from Yahweh's covenant leads to human sacrifice. Jephthah sacrifices his daughter because he feels bound to his vow to Yahweh that he would offer as human sacrifice the first person who walked through his door upon his return if God handed him victory. This unnecessary vow demonstrated his lack of faith even though God's spirit had come upon him (11:29). Therefore, the story portrays Yahweh as the One who oppresses instead of the One who delivers.

How do we respond to such an unreasonable story about God, vows, faithfulness, and female sacrifice? One way to separate Yahweh from this horrendous act is to acknowledge that Jephthah's vow of a human sacrifice was borrowed from other cultures. As New Testament scholar David Janzen points out, the story fits with the Deuteronomistic message of Judges because it shows the extent to which the Israelites have gone astray from their covenant with God. The Israelites are unable to trust when Yahweh's spirit comes to them and that it is sufficient (11:29). Instead, they cling to unnecessary signs and vows that lead to the abominable practice of human sacrifice. This story supports the Deuteronomistic theology and makes the case that Israel needs a monarchy to centralize faith in Yahweh and lead them out of this moral chaos.[1]

This understanding fits the overall narrative and purpose of Judges. Biblical scholar Esther Fuchs points out that the literary style of Jephthah's story moves the readers' sympathies to lie with Jephthah more than with his daughter. Jephthah is introduced as an ostracized, disrespected warrior when he is begrudgingly brought back into Gileadite society. Fuchs notes how the story's wording emphasizes *Jephthah's* pain when his daughter is the first to greet him. His words place the blame on the daughter. However distorted, the narrator wants us to see Jephthah as the victim and to sympathize with him. The daughter, in contrast, speaks very little. Her first words mimic Jephthah's words and accept his interpretation that the vow cannot be broken. When she submits to the sacrifice without protest, the Deuteronomistic order of God over man, man over woman is fully supported.[2] The Deuteronomistic narrator and message is primarily concerned with Jephthah who, like Israel, has been victimized, has completely lost his way, is brought to his knees, and is doomed to agony (11:35).

Fuchs builds on scholar Phyllis Trible's work in her book *Texts of Terror* that sympathizes with and mourns for Jephthah's daughter and insists that her violent death be mourned. Her presence in the sacred texts reveals the misogyny that affects not only ancient women but also women today, some of whom die through domestic or institutionalized violence.

But what if Jephthah's daughter made a conscious decision? Danna Fewell, an Old Testament scholar, suggests that Jephthah's daughter submitted to the sacrifice as a conscious choice to spare a servant that horrendous fate. By doing so, the daughter condemns Jephthah's distorted priorities, and since Israel allowed the vow to be fulfilled, she also condemns Israel. Her strength of character to condemn these priorities are consistent with her strength to request two months with her friends prior to her sacrificial death. This request wrestles the control of the situation from Jephthah and into the daughter's hands.[3]

The question, Where is God in this story? resists the misogyny in the account. God appeared in Genesis 22 and spared Isaac, the son, from human sacrifice. The prejudice of male-centered societies in ancient and modern times and the androcentrism inherent in the Deuteronomistic faith perspective is that sons are more valuable than daughters. Jephthah's daughter resisted the collusion of faith with androcentrism that gives unrestrained power to a few men over men and women who are economically and/or racially marginalized. Her resistance points to an alternative understanding of God's covenant and the reason for which Israel was chosen. In choosing to spare a servant the fate of human sacrifice, she restores the interpretation that Israel is chosen to be a blessing for all the nations and reveals a God who repudiates the thirst for genocide and revenge.

We too must resist the accepted values of androcentric religion that allow religious institutions to presume a hierarchy of relationships and ascribes it to how God relates to humanity—God is over man and man is over woman—and places all women and girls at risk. When this happens, modern communities lose their moral compass just as the ancient communities did. The answer to Where is God in this story? is that God cannot be found in this story because Israel has abandoned God. Israel and Jephthah, in spite of their altars and cries to the Lord, are acting on their own.

Samson, a Confusing and Confused Leader (Judges 13–16)

Samson is God's chosen deliverer for Israel and seems to live his calling as it fits his personal agenda. Samson is also an unwanted deliverer. In this story, unlike the previous ones, the Israelites do not cry to God to deliver them from the Philistines. On the contrary, the Israelites from the tribe of Judah take Samson and hand him over to their enemies, the Philistines (15:12-13). Samson's life and purpose seem more like a perplexing riddle than a victorious story of faithfulness to God.

The first riddle is Samson's identity and self-perception. In his birth narrative in Chapter 13, a divine messenger approaches his mother and then his father with the good news that their barrenness will end with the birth of a son who has been chosen to be a Nazirite dedicated to God (see Numbers 6:1-21). It's an auspicious beginning. His mother, who remains unnamed, immediately has easy faith and doesn't demand further proof from the messenger. She is eager to follow the dietary instructions to nurture the baby as a Nazirite. However, his father, Manoah, is slow to believe and demands proof of the messenger's divinity. As Samson grows into a man, he exhibits none of his mother's piety and fidelity to Yahweh or reverence for his Nazirite identity. Instead, like his father, he appears to be slow to understand what God has bestowed upon him.

Samson's marriage to a Philistine woman is another riddle. Even though the text reveals that the spirit of the Lord was in his decision to marry, when Samson eventually overpowers the Philistines, he does so out of personal vengeance, not for the sake of the Israelites and without acknowledging Yahweh. His selfish actions result in his wife's brutal death and place the Judahites at risk. Only after the Judahites turn Samson over to the Philistines does the Lord's spirit fall upon him. He is given the strength to overpower 1,000 Philistines. Then, only after God splits open a hollow rock filled with water to reenergize Samson, does the text offer, "Samson led Israel for twenty years during the time of the Philistines" (15:20).

This first story about Samson reveals that Samson is a leader without willing followers and a Nazirite who does not adhere to his role. Samson is also an impulsive man who feeds his appetite for sex, vengeance, and power with no thought to consequences.

Samson does, however, understand that his amazing strength is a gift from God. Unfortunately, this does not translate into a thoughtful discernment of how God would want him to use this power to deliver Israel. The fact that he overpowers the Philistines and delivers Israel seems almost an unexpected bonus of his vengeful acts.

As Samson's story continues with a new relationship with a woman named Delilah, there is hope that 20 years of leadership of Israel has matured his character and faith. But not so. Delilah, unlike Samson's wife, is introduced without any connections to male relatives. She appears to be alone. In ancient society, a woman alone is at risk of poverty, being sold into slavery, or worse. The text tells us that Samson falls in love with her but doesn't reveal whether she fell in love with him. The Philistines confront Delilah and offer her money for the secret of Samson's strength. Delilah finds herself in the middle between the Philistines and Samson, similar to the Judahites in Chapter 15. Delilah understands what the Judahites understood—that self-preservation left her no choice but to turn Samson over. But unlike the Judahites who made the same decision and are deemed politically astute, Delilah's choice has made her synonymous with betrayal and seduction.

Samson plays games with Delilah and seems delighted to make a fool of her. Every time Delilah asks the secret of his strength, he offers a false "secret" and waits for the Philistines to descend upon him so he can overpower them. With each triumph, he is arrogant about his strength. The text, with tongue in cheek, says that the physically undefeated Samson cannot stand up to Delilah's nagging. This conceals the truth that Samson gets caught up in his own power and believes that even if he tells the secret, his power will be sufficient.

This does not happen, much to his surprise; "He woke up from his sleep and thought, I'll escape just like the other times and shake myself free" (16:20). The Philistines brutalize him and humiliate him by gouging his eyes and keeping him chained. In this state, Samson finally realizes that without God, he has no power. He waits for his hair to regrow and asks God to remember him once more. He then sacrifices himself to defeat the Philistines. However, even his final act is an act of personal vengeance more than a desire for the good of Israel.

Samson as a hero of faith is a riddle. He demonstrates no leadership and is motivated by personal vengeance. The women he loves are put at risk by his presence, and he gives them no protection. His devotion to God is visible only when he is in trouble and in need of help. Nevertheless, once helped by God, Samson returns to trusting his own impulses. Samson's story underscores how much the Israelites were in need of repentance and a centralized base to anchor their covenant with God.

"In Those Days There Was No King in Israel" (Judges 19–21)

The last three chapters of Judges close the book with hopelessness and horrifying accounts of the attempted rape of men, a gang rape of a woman, rape as a military weapon, and civil war between the Israelite tribes. The narrator begins Chapter 19 with the same words—"In those days when there was no king in Israel"—and ends the book by saying, "each person did what they thought to be right" (21:25). These final chapters strengthen the narrator's case for Israel's need of a monarchy. The narrator illustrates this need by reminding the Israelites of the wretched acts they committed when they trusted their own judgment without accountability to Yahweh's covenant. The narrator refuses to keep these skeletons in the closet. The accounts in these chapters evoke shame and outrage. The Israelites not only walked away from God, but they walked away from decency and basic humanity as well.

The story of the Levite and his secondary wife begins with a marital problem. The CEB says the wife did an "act of unfaithfulness" (19:2), but the underlying Hebrew can be read as "resists him." When she leaves the marriage, she commits an unfaithful act within the Deuteronomistic hierarchy of relationships. She returns to her father's house for refuge, but her father returns her to her husband. Since she is not given a voice, we don't know why she ran away, but many scholars speculate, based on her husband's attitude in the rest of the narrative, that he was abusive.

On the way back home, the Levite and his wife are offered hospitality in an old man's home in Gibeah, in the territory of the Benjaminites. That evening, men of that city surround the house and ask for the Levite so they can rape him. Instead, the old man offers his own daughter and the Levite's secondary wife but to no avail. Nevertheless, the Levite throws his wife out the door. In the morning, he finds her dead, the result of gang rape. He doesn't seem to mourn her; instead, he mourns the injury to himself through her. He dismembers her and sends her body parts to each Israelite tribe asking for revenge against the Benjaminites. The tribes are outraged that the man has been so shamed, but there is no mourning for the woman.

When the tribes receive the Levite's message, it incites a civil war against the Benjaminites so violent that only 600 men survive (20:47-48). Suddenly, the other 11 tribes realize they have all but destroyed one of their own tribes and cry out to God in remorse. To rectify this, the tribes give amnesty to the 600 remaining Benjaminites; but since their wives and children had been massacred and the other tribes have vowed not to allow their women to marry Benjaminites, the tribe could not restore itself. The other tribes resolve this by attacking the Israelites of Jabesh-gilead, justifying it as punishment for their neutrality in the civil war. They kill all but 400 virgin women, which they hand over to the remaining Benjaminites. Since 200 more virgins were needed, the tribes instruct the Benjaminites to abduct women from Shiloh during their festival and make them their wives.

Across the Testaments

Thwarting God's Love

The story of the abuse of the Levite's wife is an example of how religious laws thwart God's love when they collude with cultural and political institutions. This problem was also evident in Jesus' day in John 8:1-11 where some Pharisees bring before Jesus a woman caught in adultery to test if he will keep the religious laws that demand stoning (death) as punishment. They literally make the woman an object lesson. Jesus, however, answers the true question behind law: How does God relate to his creation, male and female? His simple directive, "Whoever hasn't sinned should throw the first stone" (8:7), reveals the Pharisees' need for grace that was as great as that of the woman and her absent male accomplice. It liberated God's love from the chains of self-serving cultural and political agendas. God's love, embodied in Jesus' actions and words, made no distinction between the gathered men with stones in their hands and the woman they were objectifying—they were equal as God's children.

The Pharisees treated the woman no differently from how the Levite treated his wife, but in Judges, the Levite's wife does not have a savior. She dies and God's love is thwarted. Jesus' action of saving the adulterous woman answers for the Levite's wife's death. She, her husband, father, the Benjaminites, and all the tribes of Israel are beloved children of God who can be set free from sin by the grace of God and begin to live together differently.

This account of murder and rape as an act of war is told without any sense of outrage, but rather as explanation for how Israel kept its 12 tribes intact. The only rape that receives a hint of outrage is the attempted rape of the Levite man and the shame brought upon *him* when *his* wife was gang raped. But by telling these stories, the Bible bears "sacred witness to the prevalence of rape [and misogyny] in past and present lived experiences of women, children, and men. This is how biblical literature contributes to an understanding of the various settings in which we live."[4] It gives us permission as people of faith not only to protest the rapes and misogyny but also to protest when our own Christian faith colludes with a worldview that fuels such acts even today.

Live the Story

The Book of Judges is a sacred witness about the oppression suffered by men, women, and children when God's covenant of love is ignored. It helps us to protest oppression today. The horror of the stories found in the Book of Judges helps us resist the patriarchal mindset precisely because it exposes its flaws.

Happily, our sacred text does not end with this book. The Book of Ruth follows the Book of Judges and teaches us about God's love and redemption and introduces us to Jesus' foremother. God's final word is the transformation of all of our relationships as taught by Jesus.

Where do you need to stand against oppression today?

[1] From "Why the Deuteronomist Told about the Sacrifice of Jephthah's Daughter" in *Journal for the Study of Old Testament*, by David Janzen (SAGE Publications 29.3, 2005); page 355.

[2] From "Marginalization, Ambiguity, Silencing: The Story of Jephthah's Daughter " *Journal of Feminist Studies in Religion*, by Esther Fuchs (Indiana University Press); pages 35–45.

[3] From *Judges* (Fewell); page 71

[4] From *Sacred Witness: Rape in the Hebrew Bible*, by Susanne Scholz (Fortress Press, 2010); page 211.

5.

God's Love (*hesed*)

Ruth 1–3

Claim Your Story

Have you ever found yourself thinking, *I never saw this coming* or *My life is not falling into place the way I thought it would?* Unexpected events place us at difficult crossroads, sometimes causing us to ask such questions as, Haven't I been faithful? What is the best decision that is in line with my faith's values? Who is God, and does God care about me? Does God care about the lack of justice in my life and in the world? Difficult crossroads make us reassess our beliefs about religion, culture, relationships, and how life works in general.

We meet the main characters in the Book of Ruth at one of these unexpected crossroads. The very human characters in Ruth reveal the limitations of our religious and cultural systems to help us rethink and experience God. The questions Ruth poses to us are, Will I allow myself to lean forward into God's generosity and toward others with an open heart and hands in fearful times? Will I be a faithful witness of God's unconditional, unbounded, and compassionate love?

Enter the Bible Story

Introduction and Background

Ruth is a timeless "bestseller" within the biblical canon for both Jews and Christians. Its dialogue helps us hear the women's perspective and authority, even if we don't know the gender of the author. Some scholars conclude that the very existence of this novella reveals women's powerful authority in everyday life that regularly circumvented the patriarchal social structure. Ruth stands out among the biblical literature because it shows that God's message to the Jews may come directly from women and that women are capable of critically thinking about faith and life in spite of the sexism and laws that sought to limit their power and worth.

Naomi

The Book of Ruth begins with Naomi, a Hebrew woman from Bethlehem and a poverty-stricken refugee in Moab, the most despised foreign land among Israelites. She loses her husband and sons and subsequently loses one of her daughters-in-law due to the religious purity laws and economic systems.

Cleverly, this parable-style novella uses wordplay to name its characters, and in doing so, reveals to its first hearers that this story is more than meets the eye. Naomi's family reside in famine-stricken Bethlehem, which ironically means "house of bread." Her husband's name, Elimelech, means "my God is King," implying his faithfulness. For survival reasons, this faithful Jew takes his family to live among the Moabites, whom the Torah condemns as Lot's incestuous descendants (Genesis 19:30-38). Naomi's name means "sweetness." Her sons' names Mahlon and Chilion mean "sick" or "diseased." The sons eventually marry Moabite wives who are named Orpah, which means "the nape of the neck," implying that she is prone to abandon; and Ruth, which means "watering to saturation," implying that she is prone to generosity.

Thus, at the outset, the first readers would sense the prevailing religious argument that intermingling with foreigners, especially the Moabites, was an unfaithful act against God and would lead to death and sorrow. Sweet Naomi was suffering the consequences of her husband and sons' sins. Orpah's name reminds the first readers of Moab's historical oppression of Israel (Judges 3:12-15) and foreshadows her abandonment of Naomi. When the story assigns the name Ruth to a Moabite woman (typically stereotyped as promiscuous), the first hearers are caught off guard. The prevailing religious and cultural norms of how God relates to foreigners and how God desires for Jews and foreigners to be in relationship bursts wide open for collective scrutiny. The first readers see their own stories of friends and families with foreign kinships reflected in Ruth and Naomi's story.

Naomi urgently seeks her home community, Bethlehem, for economic security at the mercy of relatives. Naomi's sweetness is visible because she also desires economic security for her daughters-in-law and instructs them to return to the households of their mothers (1:8). The use of the word "mother" here is recognition of the behind-the-scenes pivotal role women played in household decisions, including marriages (see also the use of "mother's household" in the story of Rebekah and Isaac in Genesis 24:28 and in Rebekah's pivotal role in gaining Jacob the birthright over his twin, Esau in Genesis 27:5-17). The first chapter of Ruth reveals the tacit power of repressed women in a male-dominated society.

The emotional exchanges between Naomi and her two daughters-in-law are heartbreaking (1:9). The Jewish mother-in-law loves her Moabite daughters-in-law. Naomi's advice to them to return home made good sense. Their best hope was to place themselves at the mercy of their respective families instead of staying together as penniless widows. Orpah abides by the religious and economic institutions of her day when she leaves under great duress. Ruth's decision to remain with Naomi, on the other hand, is countercultural and unexpected. Her pledge is similar to Abraham's pledge to God when he left home to follow God. Ruth is behaving as a pious, faithful man whose ethics are guided by the belief that "my God is king." Her actions demonstrate that she is being excessively kind and loving (*hesed*) toward Naomi. In this way, she lives up to her name, "watering to saturation."

The first chapter ends with Bethlehem's women speaking in one voice. They remember and greet Naomi as she returns to Bethlehem with Ruth. Surprisingly, neither the women nor Naomi acknowledges that Ruth is present. More surprising is Naomi's silence about Ruth's incredible pledge of love and loyalty to her and to Israel's God. Naomi's silence hints that she is ambivalent about Ruth's pledge. Ruth, the Moabite, is both an asset and a liability to a faithful Hebrew widow. She is an asset because of her ability to work and her companionship. But Ruth is also a liability because her people are despised by the Israelites. Her presence goes against the laws of purity and makes it difficult for Naomi to be restored in the eyes of society. Despite these risks, Naomi chooses to live with Ruth. Still, Naomi has many reasons to call herself Mara, which means "bitter" (1:20).

Why Ruth May Be Read as a Parable

Reading Ruth as a parable is helpful. Parables portray the everyday life issues that concerned the people for whom they were written to reveal a new framework with which to understand their situation. Jesus used parables effectively, and like Ruth, his parables were infused with irony, satire, commentary, ambiguity, or riddles. Theologian Catherine Keller writes that in parables "truth [is] told not straight but [on a] slant.... Deliberately and simultaneously they conceal what is revealed and reveal what is concealed."[1] This is certainly true of Ruth and understanding it helps us mine its depths of seemingly paradoxical details.

The first chapter conceals the prevailing Torah interpretation against intermarriages in the implicit message that Elimelech's and his sons' deaths are God's punishment. It also conceals the prevailing Torah interpretation that repentance and restoration to proper faith is to disavow foreign family members, especially women. The story also conceals the accepted political and economic institutions that turn Naomi's, Orpah's, and Ruth's widowhood into poverty. It reveals Israel's economic oppression of women that prevented them from inheriting property, which is in contrast to foreign countries' inheritance laws. As it conceals these prevailing religious interpretations and cultural norms, it reveals a major theological debate about the nature of God. Questions arise such as, Is God a rigid, jealous deity whose demand for absolute loyalty exacts dire punishment for a man and his female relatives when they try to survive? Is God a loving entity whose mercy and compassion transcend race, gender, ethnicity, and class? How does God reveal the God-self to humanity? Is the Abrahamic blessing exclusive to Abraham's descendants, or are the descendants to be a blessing to all humanity?

The scene in the plains of Moab where Ruth offers her Abrahamic-style pledge of loyalty and love to Naomi reveals that God's presence dwells in Ruth because she is the one who bears witness to a love that overflows the boundaries of social, religious, and economic norms. God's revelation circumvents the Jews and touches Ruth directly, for it is Ruth the foreigner who has the courage to risk everything for the sake of love and not Naomi, the sweet, faithful Jew. In contrast, the story reveals that Naomi's obedience to her religious laws, influenced by social and economic pressures, *restricts* her love!

As a parable, Ruth's power for ethical-theological critique is as formidable as Jesus' parables in the New Testament.

Ruth

Ruth becomes the center of attention in Chapters 2–3, and Naomi is in the background. Ruth's actions reveal how she goes beyond what is expected for Naomi and lives up to her name, "watering to saturation." She defies the Moabite woman's stereotype as pagan, promiscuous, untrustworthy, and dangerous.

These chapters also introduce Boaz, whose name means "powerful, well-respected, pious one." Through him, Ruth will be able to enact her love for Naomi. Boaz's actions are ambiguous and scholars have read him in various ways. Sometimes he is a man who has to be shown how to become a redeemer, and other times he demonstrates *hesed* in his excessive generosity and his initiative to work around the levirate laws to help Ruth procure full redemption for Naomi. The text's ambiguity reveals that the story continues to be true to its parable form.

Gleaning in the Fields (2:1-16)

Ruth goes to the barley fields as a gleaner because this was the work allowed for foreigners. When Boaz, the landowner, arrives, Ruth is introduced by the foreman not by name but rather as "a young Moabite woman, the one who returned with Naomi from the territory of Moab... [s]he arrived and has been on her feet from the morning until now, and has sat down only for a moment" (2:6-7). It is evident that Ruth is known in Bethlehem as Naomi's foreign daughter-in-law. In the fields, however, she is recognized as one who works beyond what is expected. She is excessive in her labors just as she is excessive in her kindness, *hesed*. Ruth's character is beginning to chip away the stereotypes.

Sex and Redemption: The Threshing Floor Scene (3:1-18)

The encounter on the threshing floor transforms from a seduction for marriage to a business deal that exacts full economic redemption for Naomi. Guided by Naomi, Ruth plays the part of the seductress, but the conversation she has with Boaz quickly turns into a business deal. Ruth's power is her unwavering devotion/love *(hesed)* for Naomi's wellbeing. It would have been sufficient for Ruth to simply marry a young man for economic security and support Naomi as part of her household. Yet, Ruth desired full redemption for Naomi that required both an economic transaction to reclaim Elimelech's land and a marriage to produce an heir that would allow Elimelech's family name to continue.

When Boaz awakes to find Ruth at his side, his question "Who are you?" perhaps was a query about her character, for surely he recognized her (3:9). Ruth's response is that she is the foreigner-relative that is in need of protection and redemption. Her use of the word *kanaf*, translated as "robe" (3:9), which Boaz used in their introduction in the gleaning fields (2:12; rendered there as "wings"), shows her quick thinking. It reminds Boaz that he is in the position to give her what he prayed on her behalf—marriage (2:12). The phrase "spread my cloak" is used in Ezekiel 16:8 to mean a pledge of marriage. This phrase becomes ambiguous in this midnight meeting at a threshing floor. (Hosea 9:1 alludes to a threshing floor as a place where men meet prostitutes.) But since Ruth ends her request with the phrase, "because you are a redeemer," the original readers knew she seeks something more (3:9). The Hebrew word is *go'el*, and its translation as "act as next-of-kin" dilutes its impact for modern readers who do not understand that to act as a next-of-kin is to be a redeemer of property, reputation, and/or family name. The first readers and Boaz certainly understood that she was asking for more than a marriage proposal with *go'el*. Boaz quickly understands the extent of her loyalty and love *(hesed)* for Naomi. Ruth sought to provide an heir that would continue the family name and reclaim the family property. She hoped to give

Naomi a full restoration to what her life would have been had she and Elimelech never left Bethlehem and their sons had produced heirs.

Without hesitation, Boaz accepts Ruth's request for a pledge of marriage and economic redemption. He begins to enact a plan to overcome a major barrier that is revealed in Chapter 4.

Ruth's final words in this chapter are her last words in the entire story. When she returns home in the early morning, Ruth tells Naomi all that had transpired. Ruth again surprises the reader in her response to Naomi's question of why she has arrived with such large amounts of barley. She twists the truth to give Naomi hope. She honestly answers that Boaz generously gave her the six measures of barley, but she omits that he did so as a ruse to prevent her being mistaken as a prostitute. Instead, Ruth tells Naomi that Boaz wanted her to return to Naomi with a gift. Ruth's last words in the story are words of hope for Naomi that Boaz, her distant relative, is thinking of her wellbeing and that he will surely provide for her.

Reading Ruth Chapters 1–3 as a Parable

Chapters 2–3 continue in parable style that conceals to reveal and reveals what is concealed. The first thing that is concealed—hidden in the story—is whom God chooses to bear witness of Divine redemption. The person God chooses, Ruth, reverses humanity's religious and social norms of gender, race, ethnicity, class, and culture. On face value, the story seems to be simply about a quick-witted Moabite who, with the help of her Jewish mother-in-law, schemes to gain a husband for economic security. However, Ruth's encounter with Boaz the first day in the field is marked by Boaz's recognition of her pledge to Naomi to live with her and accept her God. His offer to Ruth of water, nourishment, and protection from sexual assault is, at first glance, a simple act of hospitality befitting a powerful, pious man. A second look indicates that the first reader undoubtedly saw the parallels between Ruth's encounter with that of Abraham's servant who journeys to find Isaac's wife, Rebekah, (Genesis 24) and of Moses' arrival to Midian and the warm reception each man receives (Exodus 2:15-22). This simple scene of Ruth's need for hospitality, water, and nourishment parallel the stories of three important patriarchs—Abraham, Isaac, and Moses. It also reveals that God chooses Ruth and Boaz, like the patriarchs, for a fresh witness of right living under divine grace.

The ambiguous conversations between Boaz and Ruth in the gleaning fields also reveal the well-known practice of raping foreign women working the fields at the hands of the male (Jew and foreign) field hands. Ruth offers an exaggerated word of thanks to Boaz when he allows her to glean in his fields and uses a word for foreigner that can also mean someone who should be recognized as a family member. Ruth implies that she needs protection, and Boaz then becomes concerned over Ruth's safety and commands that she not be "assault[ed]" (2:9). That alludes to the frequent rape of foreign women working in the fields. It also denotes Boaz's sexual interest in Ruth, revealing that even pious men are affected by stereotypes of foreigners and a patriarchal culture that sees women as objects for men's use, abuse, and pleasure. However, Boaz is able to rise above the culture's expectations of men's rights and relies on his piety to choose to act as Ruth asked that he would—as a distant relative who could protect her. Boaz chooses to counter the edicts that demand disavowal of foreign women, and instead he taps into God's bountiful love—*hesed*.

Live the Story

At a difficult crossroad, Ruth finds herself guided by the impulse to reach out with open hands to Naomi. Boaz and Naomi respond to her generosity with generosity.

Immigrants and refugees living in the West who read Ruth will identify with the fear at the crossroads of whether to return home. Most cannot because geopolitical forces have ravaged their homes. They identify with Ruth, who chooses to risk prejudice in a foreign state for the promise of economic possibilities for her family.

Farmers in the United States who legally hire Mexican field workers will identify with Boaz, who works around a broken political system with integrity to do what is right for his reliable foreign workers. Fidelity to God's love in this political and legal system is difficult.

Women also may resonate with Ruth's description of the risk of sexual assault. The 2011 PBS documentary *Women, War and Peace* notes how rape has become an acceptable weapon of war. Also, the rise in human trafficking of young girls in the United States, the pervasiveness of date rape, and incest expose women's precarious state under the veneer of Western equality.

Ruth chose to lean into God's love, *hesed*, in her difficult crossroads. Will we lean into *hesed* to bring healing to the refugee, immigrant farm worker, US farmer, and assaulted young girl? Will we choose to bring a spirit of generosity and compassion to the strangers in our midst? Will we trust God to multiply that generosity and love in the lives of others, as Ruth trusted? Will the Christian church bear witness of God's love—*hesed*? Will you?

[1] From *On the Mystery: Discerning God in Process*, by Catherine Keller (Fortress Press, 2007); page 137.

6.

We Are All Related

Ruth 4

Claim Your Story

The church I attend is similar to many congregations across the United States in its outreach ministries to its neighbors. It offers a free medical and legal clinic and has a preschool for the working poor who do not qualify for the government program Headstart. Our relationship with the city's refugee services over the years has led to many refugees joining our congregation. As a result, our membership is very diverse with people from all over the world. Many of our members are caught in the continuum of documentation with our government from undocumented, refugee, and resident all the way to naturalized and native-born citizen. Our church is not unique in the United States; many churches throughout the country bear a similar witness of Jesus' hospitality to all.

In the Book of Ruth, Boaz and Naomi have loving relationships with Ruth, resembling the relationships between our church members and the neighbors who come to our legal and medical clinics and the children in our preschool. The ethical problems that Boaz faced when standing with Naomi and her Moabite daughter-in-law are similar to those we face in light of the anti-immigrant and anti-gay sentiments in religious and political arenas. Most churches come before God prayerfully asking, How should we be faithful? In our case, God's response comes in the face of a refugee youth, gay/lesbian member, or in an undocumented patient in the clinic. They courageously offer their gifts, time, and love on behalf of our congregation, in spite of the risks and sacrifices. Their witness to God's love (*hesed*) prompts a response in kind from the rest of the members.

Leaning on one another, the diverse church members are discovering the overabundance of joy found in God's love and are building a community whose heart is like a cup running over with God's living waters.

What response do you hear from God when you personally pray the questions, How should we be faithful? What response do you hear on behalf of your church?

Enter the Bible Story

Love at Bethlehem's Gate

Boaz takes center stage after the cliffhanger ending of Chapter 3. His actions will determine whether Ruth and Naomi's hopes will be fulfilled. Boaz does not disappoint! He, like Ruth, goes to great lengths to seek redemption that is beyond what is expected of a relative.

Boaz carefully seeks elders to accompany him to the city's gate, and calls Naomi's nearest relation—who is more closely related to Naomi than he is—to a meeting. A crowd gathers to bear witness to the negotiations between two potential redeemers (go'el) for Naomi and Ruth. The reason for the meeting is an economic one: the sale of Elimelech's land. Up to now, there has been no mention of property that Naomi and Ruth could claim, so this is a twist in the story. Evidently, Boaz knows about the land, which has no doubt been taken over by squatters after Elimelech abandoned it when he took his family to Moab. Was Boaz's promise to Ruth for property gain?

The story tells us that Boaz, the pious and powerful man, follows the proper rules. He informs the nearest relative who has the first right to the land and sets up a meeting at Bethlehem's gate. The kinsman understands that claiming the land is an opportunity for economic gain, but it comes with taking on Naomi as a dependent. Since Naomi has aligned herself as kin to Ruth, it is implied that Ruth also comes with Naomi. Verse 5 in English has Boaz saying to the kinsman, "On the day when you buy the field from Naomi, you also buy Ruth the Moabite, the wife of the dead man." Naomi's nearest blood relative and proper go'el (redeemer) will not assume the political, religious, and economic risks associated with connections to Naomi and Ruth the Moabite who is a *persona non grata* in Bethlehem. His response is quite respectable because he obeys the prevailing interpretations of the Torah, of purity laws, and of cultural norms regarding relationships with foreigners. His declination was predictable given the circumstances and conditions that came with the property. Boaz knew this when he made the offer.

This scene changes how we understand Boaz, however, when we read verse 5 in the original Hebrew, which can be read as "on the day you buy the land, I will buy Ruth." In the Hebrew, Boaz does not leave anything up to chance, and he publicly claims the secret promise of marriage he made to Ruth. This makes the property deal much less attractive to the kinsman who immediately knows that if Boaz and Ruth produce a male heir, that heir will by law have greater rights to the land. Clearly, the kinsman would be foolish to take on such a risk. Either way verse 5 is translated, however, the kinsman's declination was predictable.

The lingering question is whether Boaz acted out of generosity or out of personal gain when he made his promise to Ruth. The answer is in verse 10 when Boaz reveals his intentions of divesting himself of the gains of the land through an heir. He publicly announces that any heirs produced by his marriage to Ruth will preserve Elimelech's, Mahlon's, and Chilion's names! This is extravagant redemption, and it is exactly what Ruth had asked for when she approached Boaz for marriage. Naomi now has the opportunity to be fully restored economically and socially.

Boaz's extravagant announcement and Ruth's courageous love for Naomi has transformed the Bethlehemites' perspective of the place of foreigners within their culture. Their spontaneous prayer (4:11-12) is evidence of the transformation. They no longer see Ruth as a Moabite to be dismissed as prescribed by purity laws and social norms, but rather they understand that God has chosen her to be like their faithful foremothers Rachel and Leah. Their vision is corrected by an unimaginable Divine love that breaks down their fear of the other. Instead of the impulse to hold on tightly to blessings as exclusive for the Israelites, the townspeople realize that God's love is meant for all people, regardless of economic class, race, gender, or ethnicity. What is more, they are humbled by the realization that God's blessing for the house of Israel will come through a foreigner, Ruth, the Moabite, and not the other way around. They pray for an heir, and God answers with Ruth giving birth to a son, Obed ("one who serves God"), whom she relinquishes to Naomi.

The Women's Chorus

At the end of the book, the women's chorus of the first chapter (1:19) reappears to bless Naomi and recount for her how much God has blessed her. In contrast to Naomi's silence and seeming lack of gratitude to Ruth, the women's chorus publicly recounts Ruth's loving actions and praises God. They understand that God's unfettered love has been at work through Ruth to restore Naomi to a full life. The women's chorus reminds Naomi, "Your daughter-in-law who loves you has given birth to [Obed]. She's better for you than seven sons" (4:15). The transformative power of God-as-love cannot be silenced even if Naomi is silent. Its power has unleashed itself in the lives of the townspeople, and they have a corrected vision of God's *hesed* and what it means to be faithful. This corrected vision helps them see that God's love turns their religious laws and male-centered view of life on its head.

The women's chorus overflows with praise for God's revelation through Ruth. The chorus bears witness that God claimed Ruth as a daughter and as the vehicle of redemption for Naomi and Bethlehem. When the women acknowledge that God's blessing to others has come through the faithfulness of a foreigner, they unravel the notion that God's blessing comes exclusively through Israel. In effect, they give praise for how God opened Boaz's heart to see the Divine *hesed* in Ruth's action and how God gave Naomi the courage to accept Ruth's pledge to stay together as a family. The faithfulness of Ruth, Boaz, and Naomi to God's love in times of great social turmoil and economic fear and insecurity modeled for the people of Bethlehem a new way of relating with one another. The women's chorus praised God for these mighty acts.

Reading Ruth 4 as a Parable

The conclusion of the story reveals the immorality and inhumane treatment of widows implicit in religious inheritance and purity laws when it is made known that a piece of property has been available to Ruth and Naomi from the outset that would have kept them from poverty. The elaborate transaction that Boaz enacts at the gate with the kinsman conceals how men and women are trapped by patriarchal and purity laws. The kinsman could not accept the land offer if he was to abide by the law; he was trapped. Boaz liberated himself from that same trap by stepping—at great social and economic risk—out of what was acceptable when he married Ruth and decided to preserve his relative's name and not his own.

Naomi's acceptance of Obed as her son without a word of acknowledgement or thanks to Ruth reveals the brokenness of human relations. Finally, the parable reveals the Israelites' folly of presuming to be able to contain God's revelation for only themselves. The women's chorus invokes God's continued presence throughout the story as they praise God for all the blessings that have poured down to Naomi through none other than her Moabite daughter-in-law. Ruth the foreigner's faithfulness and love (*hesed*) has brought down God's loving kindness and redemption!

God's Amazing Grace Seen Through Ruth's Witness

At every turn in the story, Ruth reveals her intent to fully restore/redeem Naomi's life to a greater "fullness" than Naomi can imagine. Ruth, the foreigner, enacts an excessive love. Ruth exhibits what Martin Luther King, Jr. called "excessive altruism."[1] King preached that God's love induces acts of excessive altruism with the power to disarm those who use their power for hatred. Ruth's love/*hesed* disarms not only Boaz but also the entire city of Bethlehem.

Hesed and excessive altruism as enacted by Ruth and Martin Luther King, Jr. is not limited to a romantic notion but, rather incorporates and faces the evil that exists in society's institutions of religion, politics, and economics. The Book of Ruth demonstrates that God's love/*hesed* is inseparable to full redemption and recovery (*go'el*) by using the word *go'el* six times in verses 9-13! It appears 85 times in the entire book.

Ruth's takes on the role of a redeemer (next-of-kin), usually a male role, on behalf of Naomi when she gleans the fields in order to provide shelter and food and later exacts from Boaz a marriage pledge and a promise that he will provide economic and social redemption.

Love that springs forth from the Divine includes full redemption—justice and mercy—in all aspects of human life, and Ruth, the Moabite, understands this intuitively. From the moment she uttered her pledge to Naomi in the middle of Moab's fields, Ruth enacted God's love as taught by the Torah. God's love flows through her and is evident in her creativity, courage, and confidence that parallel the faith of Israel's patriarchs. Ruth allows the people of Bethlehem to understand both the Torah and how God works in the world in a new light.

Boaz also demonstrates *hesed* by quickly understanding Ruth's request and accepting the redeemer role on behalf of Naomi and Ruth. Boaz recognizes Ruth's extraordinary acts as going exceedingly beyond what was expected from her (or anyone!). It seems that Ruth's love ignites creativity and love within Boaz, and he also goes beyond what is expected of him as a relative. On the surface, Boaz and Ruth's meeting on the threshing floor results in a marriage pledge and a promise to redeem property and a family name. Yet, it is so much more. Boaz and Ruth are filled with God's *hesed* that becomes a creative, flowing, courageous energy that moves them to defy culture and tradition to attain mercy and justice.

The complexity of how we are connected to each other globally in all spheres—economically, politically, socially—is an opportunity for us to overcome our fear of one another. It is an opportunity to move toward mercy and justice. Our religious beliefs about God's love for us as a human race binds us to one another as sister, brother, mother, father, aunt, uncle, cousin, niece, and nephew. We are related through God's love. This relationship as the Book of Ruth teaches takes precedence over nation-building, racism, economics, and gender roles. Ruth shows us how artificial these constructs are and that our fear is built on the confusion between what we need to make us happy and what we are told we need to make us happy.

Ruth's Original Audience

Scholars have an ongoing lively debate about when the Book of Ruth was written and for what purpose. The operative questions include, How did the text itself strike those who first read it? What life issues and God questions does the text bring forward? What or whom does the text keep hidden or repress? How does worldview/social location shape the meaning of the text and understanding of God?

The traditional dating of Ruth shows it was written before Israel was conquered by the Babylonians and taken into exile to Babylonia, around 950 B.C. Hence, the Christian Bible positions the Book of Ruth after the Book of Judges and before Israel institutes governance by kings. The Hebrew Bible places Ruth in the section called the "Writings," often read at festivals that celebrate the Torah. The early date is based on the belief that Ruth's purpose is to justify the presence of various foreigners (Tamar, Rahab, Ruth) in King David's lineage. Ruth's extraordinary and selfless love for Naomi and God is key to this justification.

In recent years, scholars have revisited the traditionally accepted early dating of Ruth in favor of a post-exilic date. Those in favor of this later date point out that the novella spends very little time discussing King David except for the genealogy verses at the end. This seems to indicate that by the time Ruth was written and circulated, King David's mixed lineage was readily accepted. Instead, they focus on the book's repetitive description of Ruth herself as "the Moabite" who represents the vilest foreigner to the Jews. These scholars also look at the multiple uses of the words go'el (redeemer) and hesed (love). The novella seems to challenge the traditionally accepted interpretation of the Torah by telling a story of a foreign woman who came to experience and be transformed by God's love at work within her. In doing so, it questions the power relationships between the Jews and the foreigners in their midst. Since the question of what to do with foreigners and particularly with foreign wives was a major controversy for Israel in post-exilic times, it's plausible to accept this later date for the Book of Ruth.

While in exile in Babylonia, Jews intermarried with non-Jews, creating hybrid families. After the exile, the returnees found themselves in a theological and ethical dilemma. If foreign relatives (women and children) were to be sent away empty-handed without any resources for survival, as their post-exilic spiritual leader Ezra demanded (Ezra 9–10), how does this fit with God's grace (hesed)? The Jews were at a difficult crossroads. The Book of Ruth shows a God whose love for all transforms injustices that creep into religious, political, and economic institutions. As a parable in post-exilic Israel, Ruth shakes up the status quo with its frank foray into the impossible ethical decisions they were facing.

The Book of Ruth teaches us that our faith must be placed in God's *hesed*. This love transforms us to understand that God's abundance is available for all, and it allows us to move forward with open hands to one another, claiming our kinship as children of God without exclusion. Ruth teaches us how God has no use for the word "foreigner"; we are all covered under God's amazing grace.

Live the Story

Naomi and Boaz's dilemma of how to relate humanely with a relative or neighbor who is a destitute immigrant seeking survival resonates with US citizens who enjoy civil rights and due legal process. Like Naomi and Ruth, some of us know about our own family's immigrant journey to the United States, fleeing poverty, wars, and/or persecution. We are, or should be, confounded by the tension between our faith's teachings and the cold rhetoric that abounds in society against the new immigrants today. In today's anti-immigrant climate, to work in support of undocumented immigrants' human rights of shelter, food, and humanitarian aid places people at risk of arrest.

In 2010, a group of ecumenical clergy and churches in Alabama united to challenge a new state law. Even though the judge upheld most of the law's tenets, the clergy stood firm against what is now the most repressive anti-immigration law in the United States. Threats of jail time did not deter them from bearing witness that the law was morally flawed and that all people are children of God and deserving of justice, not just US citizens. The clergy exposed the blatant racism and political motivations that were at the heart of this law. The clergy and churches brought attention to the legislators' refusal to make the debate about the ineffective trade policies fueling the migration and a lack of an effective work visa policy for US farmers and business owners, which enables them to legally obtain sufficient foreign laborers. The group brought to light that all US citizens are connected to the injustices toward the undocumented immigrants as farmers, businesses, schools, neighborhoods, and the local economies are now feeling its effects.

Most importantly, the clergy and churches exposed how Christians are caught between exclusionary public policies and Christian works of mercy that teach that our love for God is bound for our love for one another as taught in the Greatest Commandment and in the story of the good Samaritan (Matthew 22:34-40; Luke 10:25-37).

What changes do you need to make in your dealings with others to put the relationship discoveries from the Book of Ruth into effect in your life? What will you do now to make that happen?

[1] From *Strength to Love*, by Martin Luther King Jr. (Fortress Press, 1981): pages 35-38.

Leader Guide

People often view the Bible as a maze of obscure people, places, and events from centuries ago and struggle to relate it to their daily lives. IMMERSION invites us to experience the Bible as a record of God's loving revelation to humankind. These studies recognize our emotional, spiritual, and intellectual needs and welcome us into the Bible story and into deeper faith.

As leader of an IMMERSION group, you will help participants to encounter the Word of God and the God of the Word that will lead to new creation in Christ. You do not have to be an expert to lead; in fact, you will participate with your group in listening to and applying God's life-transforming Word to your lives. You and your group will explore the building blocks of the Christian faith through key stories, people, ideas, and teachings in every book of the Bible. You will also explore the bridges and points of connection between the Old and New Testaments.

Choosing and Using the Bible

The central goal of IMMERSION is engaging the members of your group with the Bible in a way that informs their minds, forms their hearts, and transforms the way they live out their Christian faith. Participants will need this study book and a Bible. IMMERSION is an excellent accompaniment to the Common English Bible (CEB). It shares with the CEB four common aims: clarity of language, faith in the Bible's power to transform lives, the emotional expectation that people will find the love of God, and the rational expectation that people will find the knowledge of God.

Other recommended study Bibles include *The New Interpreter's Study Bible* (NRSV), *The New Oxford Annotated Study Bible* (NRSV), *The HarperCollins Study Bible* (NRSV), the *NIV and TNIV Study Bibles*, and the *Archaeological Study Bible* (NIV). Encourage participants to use more than one translation. *The Message: The Bible in Contemporary Language* is a modern paraphrase of the Bible, based on the original languages. Eugene H. Peterson has created a masterful presentation of the Scripture text, which is best used alongside rather than in place of the CEB or another primary English translation.

One of the most reliable interpreters of the Bible's meaning is the Bible itself. Invite participants first of all to allow Scripture to have its say. Pay attention to context. Ask questions of the text. Read every passage with curiosity, always seeking to answer the basic Who? What? Where? When? and Why? questions.

Bible study groups should also have handy essential reference resources in case someone wants more information or needs clarification on specific words, terms, concepts, places, or people mentioned in the Bible. A Bible dictionary, Bible atlas, concordance, and one-volume Bible commentary together make for a good, basic reference library.

The Leader's Role

An effective leader prepares ahead. This leader guide provides easy-to-follow, step-by-step suggestions for leading a group. The key task of the leader is to guide discussion and activities that will engage heart and head and will invite faith development. Discussion questions are included, and you may want to add questions posed by you or your group. Here are suggestions for helping your group engage Scripture:

State questions clearly and simply.

Ask questions that move Bible truths from "outside" (dealing with concepts, ideas, or information about a passage) to "inside" (relating to the experiences, hopes, and dreams of the participants).

Work for variety in your questions, including compare and contrast, information recall, motivation, connections, speculation, and evaluation.

Avoid questions that call for yes-or-no responses or answers that are obvious.

Don't be afraid of silence during a discussion. It often yields especially thoughtful comments.

Test questions before using them by attempting to answer them yourself.

When leading a discussion, pay attention to the mood of your group by "listening" with your eyes as well as your ears.

Guidelines for the Group

IMMERSION is designed to promote full engagement with the Bible for the purpose of growing faith and building up Christian community. While much can be gained from individual reading, a group Bible study offers an ideal setting in which to achieve these aims. Encourage participants to bring their Bibles and read from Scripture during the session. Invite participants to consider the following guidelines as they participate in the group:

Respect differences of interpretation and understanding.

Support one another with Christian kindness, compassion, and courtesy.

Listen to others with the goal of understanding rather than agreeing or disagreeing.

Celebrate the opportunity to grow in faith through Bible study.

Approach the Bible as a dialogue partner, open to the possibility of being challenged or changed by God's Word.

Recognize that each person brings unique and valuable life experiences to the group and is an important part of the community.

Reflect theologically—that is, be attentive to three basic questions: What does this say about God? What does this say about me/us? What does this say about the relationship between God and me/us?

Commit to a lived faith response in light of insights you gain from the Bible. In other words, what changes in attitudes (how you believe) or actions (how you behave) are called for by God's Word?

Group Sessions

The group sessions, like the chapters themselves, are built around three sections: "Claim Your Story," "Enter the Bible Story," and "Live the Story." Sessions are designed to move participants from an awareness of their own life story, issues, needs, and experiences into an encounter and dialogue with the story of Scripture and to make decisions integrating their personal stories and the Bible's story.

The session plans in the following pages will provide questions and activities to help your group focus on the particular content of each chapter. In addition to questions and activities, the plans will include chapter title, Scripture, and faith focus.

Here are things to keep in mind for all the sessions:

Prepare Ahead
Study the Scripture, comparing different translations and perhaps a paraphrase.
Read the chapter, and consider what it says about your life and the Scripture.
Gather materials such as large sheets of paper or a markerboard with markers.
Prepare the learning area. Write the faith focus for all to see.

Welcome Participants
Invite participants to greet one another.
Tell them to find one or two people and talk about the faith focus.
Ask: What words stand out for you? Why?

Guide the Session
Look together at "Claim Your Story." Ask participants to give their reactions to the stories and examples given in each chapter. Use questions from the session plan to elicit comments based on personal experiences and insights.

Ask participants to open their Bibles and "Enter the Bible Story." For each portion of Scripture, use questions from the session plan to help participants gain insight into the text and relate it to issues in their own lives.

Step through the activity or questions posed in "Live the Story." Encourage participants to embrace what they have learned and to apply it in their daily lives.

Invite participants to offer their responses or insights about the boxed material in "Across the Testaments," "About the Scripture," and "About the Christian Faith."

Close the Session
Encourage participants to read the following week's Scripture and chapter before the next session.
Offer a closing prayer.

1. Learning From the Past
Joshua 1–12

Faith Focus

The second chances God gives us are opportunities to better understand who God is and how we should live in relationship with others.

Before the Session

On a large sheet of paper, make a simple timeline of Old Testament dates and events showing the approximate date of the Israelites' entry into the Promised Land under Moses (about 1250 B.C.) and the time of the exile (586 B.C.). Print the following questions on another sheet: What type of allegiance does God truly desire? Are land and prosperity the rewards for faithfulness? Is God accessible only to Jewish males, or does the Divine have covenantal relationships with women and non-Israelites as well? Was disposing of women and cattle truly what Yahweh desired?

Claim Your Story

Invite participants to share family stories about tough times (especially those that were told by older family members) or other stories that had a strong impact on the lives of family members. In what ways have we romanticized these stories? What are the myths attached to the stories? What are some of the national narratives that have shaped who we are? What national strengths and flaws are central to our identity? How does the interpretation of participants' personal family stories reveal our understanding of who God is and how we are aware of God's presence throughout life?

The Book of Joshua is a book about faith seeking understanding in the midst of impending doom—a kind of spiritual discernment notebook. In this session and the next, participants will hear the various voices that make up the collective story and expose the truths that underlie the myths we adopt about our own lives and faith.

Enter the Bible Story

On the Old Testament timeline, point out the approximate date when the people entered the Promised Land, then the time of the exile. The Book of Joshua is a compilation of various types of writing with a variety of theological perspectives, so there are counter narratives that complicate the message of hope found in God's faithfulness to Israel. Look together at the questions from the study that you posted. What do these questions suggest about the Israelites? Could we apply these same questions, with some modification, to ourselves as we look at our own culture and history?

Ask the group to read the information in the study about Joshua, as well as the descriptive passages the writer lists. How does Joshua exemplify his name? How does the name's meaning serve as a message of hope for the exiled generation? Are there parallels to exile for us today? Where do we find hope in a time of economic hardship when many are jobless and have lost their homes to foreclosure? Invite someone to describe the Deuteronomistic theology the narrator of Joshua puts forth to make sense of the Israelites' life in exile. Are there those who espouse this kind of simple faith formula? Is this formula sufficient for us today in making sense of our own reality?

Divide the group into four small teams or pairs. Assign to each one of the following: The taking of Jericho (Chapters 2–6), Israel defeated at Ai (Chapter 7), God protects the Gibeonites (Chapter 9), and the miracle of the sun standing still (Chapters 10–11). Have participants read the Scripture passages and the information in the study and respond to these questions: What is the story saying? Is this a counter story? When the group unifies, have teams respond to the questions, as well as any other information they'd like to report.

Live the Story

The writer notes that second chances are opportunities to understand who God is and to see ourselves with new eyes. But this also requires the courage both to look at uncomfortable truths and to repent from wrongdoing. How do the counter voices in Joshua disrupt the dominant voice's tendency to remember Israel's history of possessing the land by covering up its historical relationships with "outsiders"?

These passages reveal that the greatness of God is found in the power of God's love for all, not just for one group, and God's love and presence are not bound by culture or land. Invite them to read over the information in the box "(Un)Holy War." What are some examples of times when Scripture has been misused to justify subjugation of others? Are there examples participants can cite from our more recent history? How have the human desires for power and wealth worked against God's inclination for justice?

Invite the group to pray silently. Ask them to bring to mind any personal experiences for which they might yearn for a second chance. What uncomfortable truths do they need to address in order to be in right relationship with God and with others? Pray that each person will trust God's unfathomable love to lead each into new ways for living life together.

2. Expanded Horizons and a Renewed Covenant
Joshua 13–24

Faith Focus

We respond to God's faithfulness to his promises with worship and renewed covenant.

Before the Session

Head a large sheet of paper with the following question: "What are your sacred spaces?" Have felt-tipped markers available for participants.

Claim Your Story

As participants arrive, invite them to print a response to the question about sacred spaces on the sheet you posted. Then discuss the following questions together: What makes these spaces sacred to you? Which of them are not actual physical spaces but practices of peace, unity, and blessing? The writer suggests that the power of sacred spaces is found in how they help us to bear witness to God's love and justice. Has this been true for participants? How do sacred spaces help us spread God's hope for those who are hurting or who feel excluded? Can a space be sacred without being grounded in justice?

Enter the Bible Story

Invite the group to thumb through Chapters 13–19 and Chapter 21. How do they think a congregation would respond if their pastor read these chapters from the pulpit? What reasons does the writer suggest for including these tedious lists? Ask someone to summarize the Deuteronomistic narrator's central faith message. Note that this last half of Joshua, like the first, includes disruptions to this primary message. The group will now consider the stories that challenge and confront the narrator's religious and social norms.

Form teams of three persons each. In each team, assign to each person one of the following passages: the story of Caleb (15:13-19); the story of Zelophehad's daughters (17:3-6); and the story of the cities of refuge (Chapter 20). In their small groups, invite participants to read over their assigned passage and the information in the study. They can then read aloud their passage for the others and answer the following questions: How does this story challenge the dominant narrative? How does it challenge the social and political norms of the time? Are these stories calling us to examine our own assumptions about norms? Ask the group to silently read Chapter 22. Then invite volunteers to summarize this story for the group. Why do we build beautiful sanctuaries and extensive church buildings? If your church sanctuary is large and beautiful, how does it function as sacred space for participants? If your church building is aging or has many maintenance issues, how does your congregation balance good stewardship of the building with the need to further the mission of the church?

Chapter 24, the end of the Book of Joshua, is a speech where Joshua recounts the people's history with God and God's miraculous acts on their behalf. Ask a volunteer to read aloud from verse 14 to the end of the chapter. The book exposes the faith crisis experienced by the readers of the Book of Joshua as they lived in exile. Review again the dominant perspective of the narrator. Invite the group to name the three ways the disruptions reveal the forces that worked against the total rewriting of Israel's history. How do these disruptions paint a picture of God that is more expansive than the image of a warrior God? Do we live today within the covenant with God to be a blessing to all? How do our churches function as sacred spaces, not only for ourselves but also for others who may be excluded?

Live the Story

Ask participants to name and discuss times when they believe religious radicals of any faith have misused sacred texts to fit their own agendas. How might we rewrite our stories as a spiritual practice to discern what God is teaching us through difficult times? How do we build into our practices of discernment the ability to evaluate past mistakes—individually and corporately—and transform ourselves to respond in new ways? Where do participants discern that new Inquisitions are underway and against what groups of people?

Despite the fact that faith and religion are still being co-opted for sociopolitical reasons, God is at work moving us toward a love that is characterized by justice for all. Look together at the questions the study writer poses at the end of the session. Invite the group to reflect on them in silence. Then point out that the writer names as sacred spaces the various places where interfaith dialogue has sprung up in the wake of September 11, 2001. Ask them to name situations or events in our common life together that are in need of this kind of transformation and list these on a large sheet of paper. What kinds of responses to each of these situations might be transformative?

Close with a prayer that each person in the group and your community of faith might find ways to make this life a sacred space.

3. How Does God Bless Us?

Judges 1–9

Faith Focus

God is present in our faithfulness during life's tragedies and in our resistance to institutionally created problems.

Before the Session

On a large sheet of paper, print the following pattern of behavior as shown in Judges: "Israel does evil in Yahweh's sight; Yahweh gives the people into the hands of oppressors; Israel cries out to Yahweh; Yahweh raises up a deliverer; the deliverer defeats the oppressor; the people are faithful while the deliverer is alive and the land has rest." Provide paper and pencils or pens for participants.

Claim Your Story

Ask someone to briefly relate the story the writer tells about the Puerto Rican evangelist. Invite participants to tell any similar stories they may have about persons whose lives have been dramatically transformed by God's love. Then ask them to think about a dark time in their own lives—illness or death of a loved one, divorce, disappointments in their professional lives, and so forth—in spite of having accepted God's love. Where was God then? In the face of experiences like these, how does God faithfully love and bless us? Does our faithlessness lead to God's punishment, or is something else happening there? Can the group name situations when they believe religion has become a tool for oppression?

Enter the Bible Story

Review the timeframe for the writing of Judges. Like the Book of Joshua, it was written many years after the events it recounts. What does the study writer indicate might be one purpose for Judges? How does the book interpret God's covenant with Abraham and Moses? In looking at the images of God presented in the whole of the Bible, the view in Judges of a God who is faithful and will never abandon the people rings true, but the form of that faithfulness needs to be evaluated in the light of the whole of Scripture. How does this incomplete snapshot of a well-intentioned but incomplete view of God's purpose and nature allow evil to flourish at the hands of religion? Can participants think of examples in our context when an incomplete picture of who God is has allowed evil to prosper?

The theological viewpoint of Judges is quite similar to that in Joshua. To what does the Deuteronomistic narrator attribute Israel's fate? The narrator situates the stories of Judges in a literary pattern to make the case for a divinely appointed king and to remind Israel that God has not forgotten them. Invite someone to read that pattern from the large sheet of paper. Ask the group to listen for that pattern as volunteers read aloud Chapter 3:7-11 and 3:12-30. Do these early stories in Judges evoke an uncomfortable laugh for participants or some other response?

Form the group into two teams. Ask Team One to consider the story of Deborah, Barak, Jael, and Sisera in Judges 4–5 and Team Two to look at the story of Gideon in Judges 6–8. Allow time to read the Scripture passages and the information in the study, and ask participants to imagine they are a review panel asked to prepare "fitness reports" for the main characters in their narratives (Deborah, Barak, and Jael; Gideon). Each team is to provide a synopsis of their story, then present their report. What is the narrator trying to show with each narrative? In the cultural context of the time, how would the group account for the inclusion of the stories of two women, Deborah and Jael, in the book? Does the group agree that the first eight chapters of Judges lead us to a spiritual dead end? What are indications that there are those today who view God's blessing as a scarce commodity?

Live the Story

Where do participants see signs today of the view that God's blessing consists of land, prosperity, and peace? Are there any indications in our own history as a nation of the perspective that bends the covenant to fit our own desire for nation building and military power? If so, what has been the result?

Invite the group to consider again the events or dark times in their own lives, as well as dark times in our corporate life as a nation. Which tragic occurrences were consequences for actions or patterns designed to consolidate a person's or group's power and were avoidable? How might God transform such events if we can demonstrate faithfulness?

Invite the group to join together in a time of prayer. Ask participants to name ways God is blessing them. Then ask participants to bring before God in silent prayer those aspects of their lives that need transformation. Thank God for the blessings named and for the potential for change in our lives. Ask participants to include both the naming of blessings and the petitions for transformation in their daily prayers in the coming week.

4. Standing Against Oppression
Judges 10–21

Faith Focus
By telling stories of moral breakdown, the Bible exposes what can happen when we lose sight of God's teachings.

Before the Session
For survivors of domestic violence, religion is still sometimes used as a means of enforcing patriarchal norms. Be sensitive to any signs you may pick up from group members that these stories are resonating in painful ways.

Print the Faith Focus statement for this session on a large sheet of paper. On another sheet, print: "In those days there was no king in Israel; all the people did what was right in their own eyes." On a third, print the following: "Resolved: Jephthah's daughter was not a victim but a hero." You will need a large blank sheet of paper, self-stick notes, and pens for participants.

Claim Your Story
Point out the Faith Focus for this session. Keeping this focus in mind is particularly important for this session. Call participants' attention to the study writer's experiences as a seminarian with the young Puerto Rican brides. Can the group think of other examples when religious institutions buttress a destructive cultural norm like machismo by using the particular maxim that wives should be subject to their husbands? Invite participants to reflect on situations in their own lives or in our communal life that we have made ethical decisions without a moral compass, continuing to do what we think is right and ascribing it to God. What were the consequences?

Enter the Bible Story
Ask the group to silently read Judges 11:1-33. Invite a volunteer to begin a group summary by telling the beginning detail in the narrative. In turn, have other participants add additional details. Call attention to the resolution about Jephthah's daughter you posted. Number off by twos to divide the group into the affirmative and the negative teams. Give each group time to read Chapter 11:29–

12:7 and the material in the session. Have each team choose two persons to debate the posted resolution. When teams are ready, give each side two minutes to present its case and an additional minute for rebuttal. The remainder of the group will serve as audience and judges.

Debrief the debate by discussing the following questions: Which interpretation of this passage supports the Deuteronomistic theology that Israel needs a monarchy to centralize faith in God? How? What difference does it make if we view Jephthah's daughter as a hero rather than a victim? Do you agree with the study writer's conclusion about where God is in this story? Why?

Read aloud Chapter 13. What does this story reveal about Samson's parents? Divide the group into three small teams or pairs. Assign to each one of the following chapters: 14, 15, 16. Have the teams read the stories of Samson to discover what each reveals about the character of Samson and decide on a way to retell the story to the whole group. Then have groups present their stories. Would they agree that Samson is a confused and confusing leader?

What is Samson's response after being helped by God? By extension, what is Israel's response? Have participants ever cried out in despair to God for help, sensed that God responded to their cries, and then returned to life as usual without making needed changes in their lives?

Call attention to the sheet with the quote, "In those days there was no king in Israel. . . ." In the same three teams or pairs, have one team read Chapter 19, a second read Chapter 20, and the third read Chapter 21. Ask each team to summarize the episode they read. Where and about what acts does the narrator show any outrage and shame? Why? Are there ways that our Christian tradition colludes with a worldview that fuels acts of rape and misogyny today? How? How should Christians witness against such a worldview?

Live the Story

Have a volunteer read aloud the posted quote again, noting that it is the final verse in the Book of Judges. Invite the group to name incidents in our current context where acts of oppression are perpetrated against vulnerable people—perhaps the trafficking of persons for sex or for forced labor, the use of children as soldiers in Sudan, or cyberbullying of young people in the United

States. Just as the women in these texts go unnamed, so do many of these persons today.

Head a sheet with the title "Texts of Terror Today." Distribute self-stick notes and pens and invite participants to print on a note a group who is oppressed but goes unnamed or whose voice in muffled. Attach these to the sheet. Close by praying that God will guide us as we discern how best to stand up for these oppressed but unnamed persons.

5. God's Love (*hesed*)
Ruth 1–3

Faith Focus

God graciously works through willing and obedient people, regardless of their status, to accomplish God's purposes in the world.

Before the Session

On a large sheet of paper, print the open-ended prompt, "I never saw this coming. . . ." On another sheet, print these two questions: "Will I allow myself to lean forward into God's generosity and toward others with an open heart and hands in fearful times? Will I be a faithful witness of God's unconditional, unbounded, compassionate love?" On another large sheet of paper, make two columns headed with the words "Reveal" and "Conceal."

In advance, ask three volunteers to prepare to read aloud Chapter 3:1-18. Assign one volunteer the part of Ruth, one Boaz, and one the narrator. Ask them to practice reading using the Contemporary English Bible (CEB).

Claim Your Story

Invite participants to think about a time when they encountered an experience they were not expecting that changed the course of their lives. Have them jot down a phrase describing that experience on the large sheet of paper. Encourage one or two volunteers to describe that experience more fully. Look together at the two posted questions from the study guide. As the group examines the Book of Ruth, they will be considering these questions in terms of whatever lies ahead in their own lives.

Enter the Bible Story

Because of the patriarchal power structure of that time, a book bearing the name of a female has significance. The study writer observes that the first chapter of the Ruth reveals the tacit power of repressed women in a male-dominated society. How?

Ask participants to pair up and talk about the meanings of their own names or of a nickname that has been bestowed on them. What do these meanings have to say about who each person is? Does anyone have a very distinctive given name that has shaped them in some way (for example, a given name that has a unique family history)? Does someone have a name he or she has had to live up to? Refer the group to the section in the study under the heading "Naomi." Invite participants to name the characters in this book and list them on a marker-board or chalkboard. What does each name mean? How does each character live up to or illuminate his or her name?

Have someone describe and define a parable. Read Catherine Keller's words that parables deliberately and simultaneously conceal what is revealed and reveal what is concealed. In the same pairs as before, ask one participant to scan the information in the study looking for what is revealed, and the other looking for what is concealed. In the unified group, invite participants to name what they found and list these under the appropriate heading.

Ruth becomes the center of the story in Chapters 2–3, and Boaz is introduced. Add Boaz's name to the list, along with the meaning of his name. What are the ambiguities about Boaz that are revealed in the text? Have participants quickly read through Chapter 2:1-16. How does Ruth show herself to be worthy of her name? How does she show *hesed*?

Invite the volunteers you recruited to read aloud Chapter 3:1-18. Given the information in the study, what strikes you about this story? What do you observe about the character of Ruth? of Boaz? What is surprising? Have the group consider what is revealed and what is concealed in Chapter 3 and write these on the lists already begun.

Live the Story

Ruth lifts up the same issues revealed in the last chapters of Judges: a culture that imposes stereotypes on foreigners and a patriarchal society that views women as objects. In the texts of terror the group read, the results were horrific. In Ruth, Boaz takes the countercultural view of foreigners and women and acts instead with *hesed*.

Have the group silently read what the study has to say about immigrants and refugees, farmers and farmworkers, and women at risk of sexual assault and death and of being trafficked for the sex trade. How do stereotypes and patriarchal norms about women play into the experiences of these marginalized groups?

Invite the group to join in prayer using the questions in the last paragraph of "Live the Story." Begin with a time of silent centering prayer. Then pray the following:

Gracious God, whose generous and abundant love surrounds us all our lives, guide us as we seek to discern how to show that love to others. Open our hearts to respond to these questions: (*read each question aloud, allowing a time of silence after each*). May we, as a church and as individuals, bear witness to God's love. Amen.

6. We Are All Related

Ruth 4

Faith Focus

God has no use for the word "foreigner"; we are all covered under God's amazing grace.

Before the Session

On a large sheet of paper, draw a simple outline of a church large enough to print words and phrases inside.

Trying to be faithful in response to issues of undocumented persons can be difficult. Conversations can be contentious, with the honest opinions of people of faith ranging across the spectrum. Pray that you can guide a discussion that will allow everyone to have a voice while dealing sensitively and respectfully with one other.

The Song of Ruth is often used as a song of romantic love at weddings, but it embodies the understanding of *hesed*, God's faithful love. If you like, show a YouTube clip of the song. You can google "Song of Ruth" or type in "Song of Ruth– OCDA 2011 Treble" for one version.

Claim Your Story

Invite the group to imagine that the church outline represents your congregation. Who are the groups of people included as a part of your church? Does your church include children, youth, and adults? Are there people with college degrees and people with GEDs? Are there various racial or cultural groups? List any categories the group can think of. Now consider people or groups of people with whom church members interact in outreach programs. List these around the outside of the outline. Ask: How does our church act in faithful ways with those beyond our doors? How do the groups with and to whom we minister affect our understanding of how to be faithful? Encourage participants to keep in mind throughout the session the question of how we should be faithful.

Enter the Bible Story

Form the group into two teams. As Chapter 4:1-12 is read aloud, Team One will listen for who demonstrated *hesed* and how. Ask Team Two to listen for who chose to act as a redeemer and how. The writer observes that Boaz's extravagant announcement (to divest himself of the gains he might make of the land through any heirs) and Ruth's courageous love for Naomi transforms the perspective the people of Bethlehem had about the place of foreigners in their culture. How does the group respond? Is it possible that some people today hold tight to God's blessings in ways that indicate a desire to keep them exclusively for Americans? What might be some possible results if we hold on too tightly to God's blessings?

For the people of Israel, Moabites were considered the most abhorrent and hated of all foreigners. Who would participants think would fall into that category for US citizens today? What if it became clear that God's blessing for us in our culture was coming through those we most fear and hate?

Review how Boaz and Ruth demonstrated *hesed*. The study writer observes that the Book of Ruth demonstrates that God's love (*hesed*) is inseparable from full redemption and recovery—and that full redemption encompasses justice and mercy. Is it possible that embracing *hesed* might move us forward in the debate over immigration in this country? If it is true that God has no use for the word "foreigner," how might an understanding of the fullness of God's love transform our contentious debates on this issue?

Though the women of Bethlehem rejoice with Ruth, Naomi remains silent even when Ruth gives her the gift of a son and heir. What accounts for her silence? Do her actions embody the name Naomi or the name Mara?

Live the Story

Invite participants to silently read the account under "Live the Story" about the clergy and churches in Alabama. Christians are often caught between exclusionary public policies and Christian acts of mercy. Invite the group to reflect silently on that statement. Then invite volunteers to listen to the following statements and consider which one most closely reflects their own position:

- Above all, I believe Christians should consider the law of the land in responding to issues of immigration.
- Above all, I believe Christians should consider God's expansive *hesed* in responding to issues of immigration.

Ask one or two volunteers to indicate which sentence they chose and why. Encourage group members to listen with respect to one another.

The writer closes with two questions that are broader than the current debate over how to respond to undocumented persons in our midst. Have a volunteer read these aloud and encourage participants to reflect on these questions in the coming week in their prayers.

If you like, close by playing the YouTube clip of the "Song of Ruth," reminding the group that although this song is often sung at weddings, it reflects the broader idea of God's extravagant, expansive love for all of humanity.

BIBLIOGRAPHY

Bibliography for Joshua

Fewell, Danna Nolan, "Joshua" in *The Women's Bible Commentary*, edited by Carol A. Newsom and Sharon H. Ringe, Louisville: WJK Press, 1992.

Jones, Serena and Paul Lakeland, "God" in *Constructive Theology: A Contemporary Approach to Classical Themes*, Minneapolis: Fortress Press, 2005.

Jones, Serena and Paul Lakeland, "The Theories of Derrida and Levinas" in *Constructive Theology: A Contemporary Approach to Classical Themes*, Minneapolis: Fortress Press, 2005.

Knight, Douglas A., "Joshua" in *The New Interpreter's Study Bible*, edited by Walter J. Harrelson, Nashville: Abingdon Press, 2003.

The Onaway Trust, "The Story of the Taino Indians of Cuba," *www.onaway.org/indig/taino2.htm*.

Bibliography for Judges

Craigie, P.C., "The Song of Deborah and the Epic of Tikulti-Ninurta" in the *Journal of Biblical Literature*, 1969.

Fewell, Danna Nolan, "Judges" in *The Women's Bible Commentary*, edited by Carol A. Newsom and Sharon H. Ringe, Louisville: WJK Press, 1992.

Fuchs, Esther, "Marginalization, Ambiguity, Silencing: The Story of Jephthah's Daughter," in the *Journal of Feminist Studies in Religion*, Bloomington: Indiana University Press.

Janzen, David, "Why the Deuteronomist Told about the Sacrifice of Jephthah's Daughter," in the *Journal for the Study of Old Testament*, London: SAGE Publications 29.3, 2005.

McNutt, Paula M., "Judges" in *The Interpreter's Study Bible*, edited by Walter J. Harrelson, Nashville: Abingdon Press, 2003.

Sirleaf, Ellen Johnson, Nobel Peace Prize Lecture, *http://www.nobelprize.org/nobel_prizes/peace/laureates/2011/johnson_sirleaf-lecture_en.html*.

Scholz, Susanne, *Sacred Witness: Rape in Hebrew Bible*, Minneapolis: Fortress Press, 2010.

Bibliography for Ruth

Brenner, Athalaya, editor, *Ruth and Esther: A Feminist Companion to the Bible* (second series), Sheffield: Sheffield Academic Press, 1999.

Farmer, Kathleen R., "Ruth," in *The New Interpreter's Bible Study Bible*, edited by Walter J. Harrelson, Nashville: Abingdon Press, 2003.

Grau, Marion, "Divine Commerce: a Postcolonial Christology for Times of Neocolonial Empire," in *Post Colonial Theologies: Divinity and Empire*, edited by Catherine Keller, Michael Nausner and Mayra Rivera, St. Louis: Chalice Press, 2004.

Jill-Levine, Amy, "Ruth" in *Women's Bible Commentary*, edited by Carol A. Newsom and Sharon H. Ringe, Louisville: WJK, 1998.

Keller, Catherine, "On the Mystery: Discerning God in Process," Minneapolis: Fortress Press, 2008.

La Cocque, Andre, *Ruth: A Continental Commentary*, Minneapolis: Augsburg, 2004.

Meyers, Carol, "Returning Home: the Gendering of the Book of Ruth" in *Feminist Companion to Ruth*, edited by Athalya Brenner, Sheffield: Sheffield Academic Press, 1993.

Pui Lan, Kwok, "Finding Ruth a Home: Gender, Sexuality and the Politics of Other," in *Postcolonial Imagination and Feminist Theology* (Louisville: WJK 2005).

Available at Cokesbury and other booksellers   AbingdonPress.co

CPSIA information can be obtained at www.ICGtesting.com
Printed in the USA
LVOW13s0119110714

393772LV00002BA/3/P